DEDICATION

My sons are my foundation, my inspiration and my joy. It is my goal also to be theirs and their families'. My sister and her family support and love me and tell me I'm wonderful in ways that I end up believing. Dear Dede, you are a tenacious encourager. Heartfelt appreciation also goes to the church people who listen to my stories and my songs before anyone else, broadening their definitions of ministry to include these things. Group, I love you. You are a ribbon of love that winds through every day. Most of all, thanks to my beloved partner Kiya. I hope she has time to listen to me tell her all the ways she warms, eases and illuminates my life. It should take forever.

CONTENTS

ACKNOWLEDGMENTS

Deep thanks to all those who have encouraged me as a writer, a preacher, and as a singer-songwriter. In my opinion, editing is also encouragement, and I want to say how much I appreciate Chris Walton, editor of *UU World* and uuworld.org for his help and support over the years my columns have been running in that magazine. Any embarrassing errors left in this book are not his fault. I would like to thank Betsy Teter, my first editor and one of the founders of Hub City Writers Project, who gave me permission to reprint *Freedom, You Do It When You Do It, Bug Zapper, Cussing, Temple of the DMV* and *Wish You Were Here* from *Return of Radio Free Bubba.*

BROKEN BUDDHA

"Broken Buddha" is the title of a photograph in my online art collection. It shows the lap of a painted statue. One graceful hand has broken off and is resting on the sole of an upturned foot. I'm trying to figure out why I'm so drawn to this image. The enlightened one as imperfect, cracked, and chipped—maybe that is how my enlightenment feels. It is not all that shiny anymore. A piece or two might have gotten knocked off.

I don't know why it makes me remember a woman—we'll call her Julie Gates—who was a pillar of my husband's Presbyterian church. Tall, slender, righteous well put together in pumps and pearls. Julie was a community saint and icon who had founded "Senior Communications," connecting the elderly all over town. Whenever her name was mentioned, someone would breathe out reverently: "Oh, she is wonderful," and everyone around would nod with downcast eyes and soft faces. She and her husband were to leave that church within a year because it "wasn't Christian enough."

"How are you enjoying being a mother?" she asked me. We had two small boys, one maybe five years old and one still a toddler. My husband, the minister, was gone a lot, and I was juggling a therapy practice, mothering, and being a writer.

"I love it," I said, "I mean, I'm tired of changing diapers, but the rest is great." It's the kind of thing parents say to one another to make the connection of telling the truth about one's life. Most people would touch your arm with a warm smile full of understanding and your hearts would beat together for a moment leaving both of you strengthened.

She did not touch my arm. She fixed me with an intense gaze and said, "I loved changing diapers. I loved every minute of raising my children. Every. Minute." My heart sank. I don't know what her heart was doing. I couldn't feel her heart anywhere. There is nothing crueler than suggesting to a young mother that she is not a good one. She quietly suspects that's true every single day of her life. I say "my heart sank," but that is only half the truth. It sank into a fighting stance with both hands raised.

This particularly crappy combination of sweetness and meanness had been coming at me from church people since I was eight years old. There was a line to toe; there was a circle of approved thoughts and behaviors within which to stay if you were to be a member of the group in good standing. If it looked as though you were about to stray, the enforcers descended with that exact tone. "Oh, you don't think that," they would say with a tinkling laugh. A spiritual person was supposed to be "victorious," triumphant in the conquering of life's difficulties, praising God in the midst of any circumstance, grateful for whatever came, peaceful in the heart, always. If you didn't feel it, by God you should just act as if you did, or it would spook all the other horses in the pasture.

The broken Buddha says I don't have to be scared of being the way I am.

I've met some non-Evangelicals with that same cruel but somehow comfortable worldview. As a practicing therapist I met a lot of people who trusted in therapy. They would speak as if you could "get help" for any situation and handle it with your head held high, your intellect clear, and your feelings in good order. If you get healthy enough you're supposed to be able to go through even a nasty divorce with peace in your heart. If something disturbing disturbs you, you should get help.

The broken Buddha tells me that sometimes agony is appropriate.

The part of me I'm least proud of imagines that this Buddha's hand detached when he reached out to someone who said something on the order of "Everything happens the way it should" and slapped them silly. In a dream workshop I was leading, an older woman was sharing her grief at having lost her son in his 20s to melanoma. They hadn't seen it because it was under his hair. A woman across the table tilted her head and spoke in that breathy voice that some people feel makes them sound more spiritual. Her eyes were wide too, and she didn't blink. "Have you ever thought about why he might have wanted to draw that suffering into his life? Why you might have wanted to draw it into yours? "

The broken Buddha tells me that life is not neat.

Life is gorgeous and horrific and beyond understanding. We may create certain situations, draw certain things, but other suffering strikes like a tiger from the tall grass, snatching us from one life into another without cause or warning. I meditate on the broken hand of the Buddha and it comforts me. It tells me that the spiritual moves in and through cracks and gaps, that it is wild and doesn't make sense. It sits with you even through something that can't be fixed by intelligence or kindness or love.

Curious about the statue, I learned that his broken hand is in the *Karana Mudra*, the shape used for warding off demons.

"The enlightened one is still whole," one of the comments under the photo reads. Someone was made nervous by the Buddha's broken hand. The one who wrote that comment wants it to be true but he doesn't know. Maybe you can be enlightened and broken too. Sometimes I feel like I understand so much, that I can be a lot of help to people. Other times my mind is blank and there is nothing in my mind or heart to say but "I'm so sorry." I want to reach out but my hand is lying in my lap, still in a shape of warding off demons of fear and illness, financial terrors and loss, and I can't do anything with it.

The broken Buddha says he knows how I feel. Our hearts beat together for a time, and we are both strengthened.

WHAT IF YOU FELT LOVED?
❖

I didn't even make a New Year's resolution last winter. I'm not sure why. For the last ten years or so my resolutions have been very short, and they have come to mind, one by one, in late December. The first one was "Tell the truth." I never thought I didn't tell the truth, but as I tried to keep the resolution on a moment-to-moment basis, I realized how much a sweet small lie lubricates social interactions. I found a way around those and counted down the months till I could indulge in them once again.

About some things, you just have to lie. Clog dancing, for example. I had someone ask me once how I liked clogging. (I was living in the Appalachian region at the time, and there is a good bit of it going on at fairs and festivals.) I answered that clog dancing held a special place in my heart. It does: the place where I imagine hell, if there were one, and what it would be like. For me it would be filling out paperwork while a flatbed truck full of white people clogged in the background to a speeded-up track of "Give Me That Old-Time Rock and Roll."

Telling the truth was what I paid attention to that whole year, discovering that my untruths mainly consisted of lies I told to myself.

"Be quiet" was the next year's resolution. It floated into my head during prayer and meditation. I did an inner double take. "What? I make my living speaking. How can I be quiet?" The Universe responded with—well, with quiet. I had to figure it out. It turned out that I needed to pay attention to being quiet inside, to not having to have an answer for every question I was asked, to being content to let others dominate a group discussion, to not voicing every opinion that was in my head.

Over the years there have been some easy resolutions and some hard ones. Who could have known that the year I resolved to "enjoy life" would turn into one big challenge? There you go. The Universe/God/Spirit/Wisdom is like that sometimes.

This year no resolution came to mind. I've been working on a question, though: "What would it be like if you felt really loved?"

Maybe the resolution is to wonder about this question. When I feel loved, my mind breathes better. My body relaxes. My behavior steadies.

Something in my spirit opens like a rose. I want to feel it if I can, from the people around me or from the Spirit of Love that flows like an ancient river through the universe.

On my first CD I printed a quotation from a letter Martha Graham sent to Agnes de Mille. According to Agnes de Mille: "I was bewildered and worried that my entire scale of values was untrustworthy. . . . I confessed that I had a burning desire to be excellent, but no faith that I could be. Martha said to me, very quietly, 'There is a vitality, a life force, an energy, a quickening that is translated through you into action, and because there is only one of you in all of time, this expression is unique. And if you block it, it will never exist through any other medium and it will be lost. The world will not have it. It is not your business to determine how good it is nor how valuable nor how it compares with other expressions. It is your business to keep it yours clearly and directly, to keep the channel open.' "

When I feel loved, it's easy to keep the channel open, and that's really what I want. Maybe I could get really good at loving the world just every other day. Maybe on that day I could love myself as well. Just every other day, let go of self-improvement and challenging other people's mistakes. I invite you to think about doing this, too. Every other day, maybe we could let go of wondering if we are good enough, of wondering if we are doing it right. Every other day rest, if we can, in the warm animal pleasures of wind, water, food, earth, friends, love, and beauty. Every other day put in abeyance the drive to feel that we are smart enough, thin enough, cool enough, doing enough.

The reason I wonder about doing it every other day is that, having read Kant, I have to ask what the world would be like if all of us did this every day. I'm not sure how well it would work. Maybe we would melt into self-satisfied goo. One the other hand, the world would be sour and clammy if we didn't do it at all. So, on alternate days we can all agree that this is New Age pap, and we can sharpen our intellectual claws in ourselves and one another with edgy glee.

I'm growing aware that I do have a resolution for the year: I get to wonder about love. Maybe being grounded in love makes change easier, rather than lulling us into staying the same. Maybe if we felt safer we would grow more freely. What if we felt really loved? This year, I mean to find out.

FRED'S FREEDOM

It's a freezing morning, and the stray puppy who wandered into the yard with his mama is howling in the dark of our garage. We caught him and put him in a huge crate with food, water, and blankets. We couldn't catch his mama, who is part Chow. She is pacing back and forth in front of the closed garage door, a foot of cheap rope handing from her collar, frayed from where she chewed through it. The puppy's collar was too tight on its neck, and neither dog had tags. They have a connection with one another, that's obvious. That is why we think the older female is this puppy's mother, although we named her Fred in the first five minutes before we figured that out. She's pacing back and forth, as I said, not with slow deliberate strides, but with running arcs. Her distress is palpable. I want to find out who owns them. It's not such a good home, that place where they let the puppy's collar get so it was digging into the flesh of his neck, where they tied up the bigger dog with rope.

I have taken pictures of the mama, printed them out big and posted them all over. "FOUND," it reads in big letters, then her picture, then my phone number. People have been calling to say they have seen that dog out running their neighborhood for a couple of days, and I needed to come get it. I explain that I FOUND that dog and I'm looking for who owns it.

The child in me wants this to be a Disney movie where the intrepid Fred finds her way home with her puppy. Maybe she finds a better home. The child in me wants to let them go to roam, roam until they find their happy ending. The adult in me knows what the world is like for stray dogs. Our two dogs got loose and traveled five miles from home. Animal Control picked them up, and I was glad. Here is how the Universe teaches me. I go through clusters of experiences. What I learned from the first one, I'm supposed to use in the next one, connect the dots.

I call Animal Control because if I were Fred's owner, that's what I would want me to do. I have a faint hope that they will be claimed. A fainter hope that they will be adopted together. A fair certainty that the puppy will be adopted, but not Fred.

Freedom brings danger. Me? I prefer freedom. Do I have the right to choose that for another being? Before my dogs got out, I would have been for letting the other dogs just go, find their way, try their luck, be free. Now, I choose safety for Fred and her puppy. Maybe safety will lead to her death. I know I am not the one who controls that. I control so little. I have to do the right thing, the next thing and leave the end of things to luck, to God, to the forces of life. I've got my fingers crossed for Fred. Wish her luck.

YOU DO IT WHEN YOU DO IT
❖

Spring is a time when everything comes around again, looking new, even though we have all seen it before. Insights are like that too. Sometimes they just have to bloom again, and you realize you had forgotten something that was really important, but here it is again.

I have been in a serious writing slump. I haven't been doing enough nothing -- just sitting around reading, or puttering in the yard. Those things free my mind to remember, to enjoy, to create. I don't think that's the real reason, though. I've had church work to do, newsletter articles and tons of email and sermons, but that's not the real reason either. The real reason I haven't been writing is that -- I haven't been writing. It has burst on me like a revelation. I do what I do, and I don't do what I don't do. I feel embarrassed by this, as if everyone on earth knows this except me. The way to write more is to turn on the computer, sit in front of it, and write.

Natalie Goldberg, whose books on writing I have read over and over, says she writes pages of something every morning, even if it's pages of "I don't know what to write, I can't think of a thing to write." In my mornings I get up, wake up my son, fix coffee, take him to school, go to drink coffee with my friends, then go to work. I have acted like I couldn't write pages in the mornings, so I couldn't write pages in the mornings.

My therapist used to ask, when I said I couldn't figure out how to make something happen, "If I paid you a thousand dollars to figure it out, do you think you could?" An answer would spring to mind. "Yeah, of course, now if you paid me a thousand dollars I could do it!" I heard his voice asking that question. I realized I can write pages any time. That it is in sitting down and writing that I make writing happen. OH.

This is the secret to eating right and exercising too. I do what I do and I don't do what I don't do. I can plan to eat more fruit and vegetables. I can buy them at the store. That is not enough to get it done. I have to actually eat them instead of eating something else. I can plan to exercise. I have planned to do yoga for about six years now. Last year I bought a mat. A friend made me some tapes. I am not feeling stretched out, strengthened, balanced. I may have to actually do the yoga to reap those benefits. If thinking about being healthy would make a person healthy, I would be walking around in a golden glow of health and good energy. People talk about getting their spiritual life going, but talking about it doesn't make it happen.

I do what I do and I don't do what I don't do. That's my new philosophy of life. My big insight. I think the Buddhists have been saying that for years. I vaguely remember learning something like that in my reading. But you know reading something and realizing it in your belly are not the same thing. Anyway it seems like the Buddhists get all the good insights first. It makes me feel a bit surly, if you must know. They are so calm and patient, and they nod when you have a realization and they don't say things like "I've been trying to tell you that all along!"

Some people, when they find out I'm a writer, say something like "I know I have at least one novel in me, I just have to let it out."

"Sit down and do it!" I say. Sometimes they think that is encouragement. It is, in a way. But it's also a declaration of hopelessness, a sure knowledge that the odds are good that they will wait for inspiration. That's a sure way not to write anything. Or they will wait until the house is cleaned up, or until they have a studio set up, or a new computer.

Those are sure ways not to write anything. I know. I've tried them all. Sitting down and doing it is the secret to writing. This morning I remembered that.

Wish someone would pay me a thousand dollars.

LETTER TO A NEW PARENT
❖

A friend of mine is going to have a baby, a little boy. My two boys are tall and funny and heartbreakingly themselves—and nearly gone. I feel like I know something, which is a fairly new feeling for me on the parenting front. Even though he did not ask me for any advice, here's what I wrote to him:

I do not know why people try to scare you when you have a baby. As soon as they hear your news they go unswervingly to the horror stories. They've probably been scaring the baby's mother for months now with stories of pregnancies gone wrong. If they can't think of bad-seed kid stories, they say, "Wait until you have a teenager!" I want to tell you something a little different. Have fun is what I say. Enjoy this baby and enjoy your newly expanded heart.

The first thing that happened when my first son was born was that I fell in love so hard and fast it took my breath away. It was enough for me to sit and stare at him, smelling his head, watching his breathing, drinking in the fact of his presence on the planet. I carried him around like a delightful football everywhere I went. Any which way I carried him was fine with him, because he was as in love as I was. Plus I had milk, which made him very happy. We hung out and smooched and sang and did "baby-cize," where I would touch his toes to his nose and count, which made him laugh.

It wasn't all bliss, of course. There was that time he was up in the night for the fourth time, crying. Babies have no manners, and they do not care about your getting enough sleep. I remember waking my husband, telling him I had a sudden fantasy of opening the window and tossing the baby out, just to get some rest. "I'm up," he said. "You sleep."

Babies are fascinating, and they're an astonishing amount of work. They get even better as they get older. They start talking, for one thing. That's a big milestone. They ask questions, start practicing "no," and they tell you they love you. That makes your life rich.

Another milestone was when he could climb into his own child seat, ending the lifting, bending, and buckling. He did not like that seat when he was smaller, and several times I would have to stop the car and rescue him as he was hanging head down into the floorboards, screaming with frustration, his ankles being the only part of him that was still in the seat. One long ride, I remember having a bag of red balloons next to me in the front seat, blowing one up, holding it so he could see it and grab for it, then letting it go whistling out the window, which made him laugh. We left a trail of deflated red balloons down Highway 17 that day. My apologies to the cleanup crew: It was red balloons or screaming insane despair. Mine and his. Is that too strongly put? No.

Getting himself dressed was another milestone, then, much later, doing his own laundry, followed by driving himself to school. Now he likes rock climbing and hard-core drumming, he's dressing himself every day, studying to be a doctor, designing his own tattoos, loving a young woman so hard they're talking about marriage. I still look at him and see that baby, the toddler, the skater-punk eleven year old.

Your baby will be who he is from the moment he comes into the world. He will turn out a little like you and a little like his mom and a lot like who he already is. You're right about the child-rearing project being improvisational from the first moment. My mother told me to trust my instincts instead of books, but I did find two that were helpful. Children the Challenge, a book from the

'40s about how to avoid power struggles with your child. You say things like: "You may scream like that if you want to, and I'll sit with you out in the car, or you may speak quietly and stay with everyone here in the restaurant," or: "It's time for bed now. Would you like to go right now or in about five minutes?" The other one was How to Be Your Dog's Best Friend, a book about training German shepherds by the monks of New Skete. It was about how your job was to make your child/dog/whichever a pleasant companion in the world, which takes patience, consistency, and boundaries. I see shocked faces when I say that a book about dogs helped with my boys, but lots of the same things are true for humans and dogs. Instead of only correcting them when they do wrong, you try to "catch" them doing it right, and praise them for that. They like knowing who is in charge, and they'd rather it be you than have to be in charge themselves. I learned that from the monks.

I worried some about my sons getting hurt. I worried more about them becoming fearful. I remember letting my younger son climb up on a chair to turn on the light by himself. I watched and held my breath. What if he fell? I figured out that making him fearful in the world would be a more severe injury than a bruise or even a broken bone incurred while trying out something for himself.

As the boys grew, they wanted to chatter to me about their toys, their friends, their video games. They wanted to retell the movies we'd seen. It tried my patience sorely sometimes, but I would say to myself: "This is an investment in their talking to me when they are teenagers. If I don't want great hulking teens who just grunt as they pass me in the hall, I need to listen now." At the supper table, when they wanted to be excused to go play, I would ask them first to ask each person at the table two questions and listen to the answers. Mostly they asked, "How was your day?" and, "Tell me who you talked to today." My oldest surprised me one night with a phone call from college to thank me for teaching him to ask questions. He said he had no problem talking to girls the way some guys at school did; girls loved that questioning and listening thing.

I used to wish my children were a little less strong-minded and independent, a little more perfectly obedient. Now that they are grown I'm glad they have their strong-mindedness. I did not enjoy their arguing with me, but I tried to think of it as training in negotiation, which they need in the world.

When you become a parent, you have to get used to making mistakes. When you make one, it's no big deal. Just say you're sorry. They learn that from you. They also learn please and thank you by hearing you say please and thank you to them. I have seen people being rude to their children, then turn around and expect the children to have good manners.

Your son will make mistakes, too, as he grows, and some of those will make you cry. Being a parent is not for the faint of heart. Try to be in control of yourself rather than of him, and you'll be okay. Love is hard on the heart. Your heart can't remain perfect and proud, unscarred and perky. It will be worn and joyous, wise and beat up, and full of sorrow and amazement. It will tremble with the awful knowledge of how helpless you are to keep him from pain, of how closely he will watch you to see what to become and what not to become. I would rather have this heart than the one I had before the first baby.

All of this is to say you are in for quite a ride. Buckle everybody up, feel the wind in your hair, and crank up the music. Enjoy. Life has just gotten larger.

CHAOS CATS

❖

My friend Henry's large orange cat is used to sleeping on the sofa. The sofa was a hand-me-down butter-yellow leather, soft and nap-worthy. Apparently the cat thought so too, because every time I went to his house, the cat was asleep on it. Henry told me the other day that he'd bought a new sofa, and the cat is not allowed on this new one. It's not a hand-me-down; he bought this sofa for himself. This is his grown up sofa, he said, and it is seriously nice, less easy to wipe off than the yellow leather. Cat hair must not be on this sofa; it has to stay pristine.

The cat is not grasping this new rule. Henry said he was tired of shooing him, yelling, waving his hands, and making dramatic assertions that he is in charge and the sofa must be respected. Still, he comes home to the sight of the cat curled up on the sofa, opening one insolent eye at the sound of the door, then closing it again. I was surprised when Henry told me he had resorted to setting mousetraps on the sofa to discourage the cat. Not the metal ones, plastic ones, but mouse traps nonetheless. The cat is fine, don't worry. He has learned to nudge each mouse trap with his paw until it snaps shut, then he pushes it off onto the floor, and when he has cleared a space, he curls up and waits for Henry to come home so he can pretend to be asleep. The power struggle continues. Maybe it's just a difference of vision about the purpose of a sofa; maybe it's more personal than that. I don't know.

I find parallels with my work life. Sometimes people get so intent on their particular idea of how things should be that they set up long lists of rules. Getting more adamant than they ought to when they talk about it, they often are willing to hurt someone else just to get things to the way they "should" be, which feels like much the same thing as setting mousetraps all over the new sofa. It could be about what kind of music is appropriate for worship services. Maybe there's a new Sunday school building, and people complain about children being all over it making messes. Maybe it's a new carpet or a new organ or maybe it's a book discussion group or a camping program. Maybe one person implies that the lady who disagrees with her about how the church library should be set up is a control freak and always needs to get her own way. Maybe the lady hints that the first person is of low character and if it were up to her she would watch out that books don't start to disappear. You know how it goes.

In any organization there are tasks that need to be accomplished, dreams being brought to fruition, challenges being met, relationships being forged and then tested. It's a spiritual exercise to balance getting the jobs done with keeping the relationships sweet and strong. We try to do a good job of balancing kindness with responsibility. Sometimes we forget, and we get too structured or too loose. Martin Luther used to say that humanity was like a drunk trying to climb up on his donkey to ride. First he falls off on one side, and then he climbs back up and falls off on the other.

In a family, at work, at church, we all have ideas about how things should be. Are you a sofa-with-cats person or do you come down strongly in the cat-free sofa party? I don't think the chaos cats care – they just want to remind us that trying to control what cannot be controlled is a shortcut to insanity. The chaos cats are wily; it is likely that they will spring our traps with impunity and lie in wait just to show us who's in charge, one yellow eye open to see if you'll get it this time.

THE DEVIL AND MARTHA STEWART

Years ago I asked for Martha Stewart's gardening book for Christmas, and I devoured it. The photographs of peonies and okra were luminous. Her garden in the winter, under snow, showed patterns of stone walls, brick walkways, hand built trellises, a gazebo, and an herb garden in a knot pattern. Month by month she instructed me what to do, from how to start seedlings to how to paint concrete urns to look like verdigris copper. She taught me to prune trees and to make a poached pear dessert with the pears that came from my . . . Well, I didn't actually do that. All I had in my garden were tomatoes, beans, and zinnias. I was a long way from pear trees.

I wondered how she did it all, and I was feeling clumsy and inadequate until I learned she sleeps four hours a night and has a staff of helpers standing by to follow her every instruction. I had no helpers, two toddlers, and my garden wasn't my paying job.

I'm not here to trash Martha, bless her heart. I just want to look at how she affects some of us. As a practicing family counselor for twenty years, I know that there is a non-rational drive in many of us to try to be perfect. It comes from the fear we all carry of not being good enough—that there is something secretly wrong with us that is not wrong with anyone else, a deficit we must cover and adjust for in all our interactions. It can drive us to try to control everything around us, to make everything and everyone do just right.

Perfectionism makes us weak—rigid, exhausted, afraid of trying something we don't already know how to do and more critical of ourselves and others than we should be. We either drive ourselves cruelly or we give up.

Martha made me feel clumsy and incompetent because I was comparing my insides to her outsides. I didn't have all the information. We know how unruly, unkind, and inadequate we are because we see ourselves inside and out. Mostly we only see other people's outsides. We don't know their private, internal struggles.

Martha Stewart is not the problem here—it's the devil. I know that's an unusual thing to hear from a rational person. Let me explain. "Satan," in the

Hebrew, means "the accuser." When I say the devil is the problem, I'm talking about that voice inside most of us that whispers, "You are not quite adequate. You're a weak specimen, a broken reed, a slight disappointment to your mother and father. You have a shameful laziness, and you might be just a touch stupid."

Do you know that accusing voice? That is the voice that fuels the fires of perfectionism—especially here at the holidays, when we want our home to be in perfect order, decorated with taste and élan; when we want the food we make to be gorgeous and nutritious and all family interactions to be respectful and loving. That accusing voice will find plenty to go on about.

What I want to say is that I think "the devil" is that spirit of fear that drives us into crabbiness and anxiety. It saps our good will and clouds our compassion. The spirit of love is where our allegiance lies as good people, soulful people, people who want to make the world a better place. Love is always in dialogue with fear in our spirits and bodies and minds. Let love win.

I will let my heart be a pear orchard. I will make my conversation with friends and family as sweet as grilled peaches. I must say "no" to the perfection, but thanks for the beauty, Martha dear.

A GOOD TREE FOR THE SEASON
❖

Our friend James died in the summer after a long struggle with cancer.

His wife said the first sign that something was wrong was when he tossed a pebble at a cardinal that was fighting its reflection in the side mirror of their Buick. The bird was chipping the paint on the car with its beak, and they couldn't figure out how to get it to stop. James tossed the pebble to scare the bird away, and his arm broke. The long, hard job of being sick started right then.

She was by his side the whole time, pushing for him to get every treatment, wishing, yelling, wanting a cure—it seemed to her—more than James did. James was pretty easygoing about most things, but she felt he shouldn't have been easygoing about dying. He was also quiet, funny, handsome, and famous for being a good kisser.

The first Christmas without James, the whole idea of family, faith, and cheery songs sung by rosy-cheeked carolers made her so mad she felt like her hair was on fire. Her teeth were gnashing and the pain in her heart clawed to get loose. One cold afternoon in early December, she bundled up and marched out the door. In the biggest box store in town, lit by fluorescent lights, trashy canned music making a mockery of the season, she stomped up and down the aisles until she saw her Christmas tree. White plastic needles held on for dear life to a bent aluminum frame. Gobs of scabrous fake snow clumped on a few of the branches. On a clearance table were a couple of boxes of dull mud-colored balls, a color between brown and gray. They were too big for the white tree. It would look awful.

She dragged her purchases back to the house, clenched her teeth, and set them up. The gray-brown balls weighed the tree down; the whole thing looked downcast and ashamed of itself. A few wads of tinsel tossed at it contemptuously, and she was through.

The spectacle gave her a snarky satisfaction every time she passed the living room. It was ugly, wrong, out of proportion, unbalanced, bedraggled, and assaulted by clumps of snow, wads of tinsel, and dull off-color balls. Perfect.

At some point she found herself walking past it because it mirrored her so well. The ironic remove, the arch sense of playing a game with Christmas, faded. The tree was her heart, and her heart was downcast, ashamed, unbalanced, and bedraggled. One day she went into the room and sat down. The tree kept her company. They made it through Christmas together, my friend and that tree.

When I was training at Walter Reed to be a hospital chaplain, one of my mentors told a story about prisoners of war on a long forced march without enough food or water. An elderly priest was having trouble, falling farther and farther back in the line. A younger man walked beside him. "I don't think I'm going to make it," said the priest.

"I may not make it either," said his friend.

Lying on the ground at night, hungry and thirsty, the priest said, "This is awful."

"Yes," said the younger man. "It's terrible, what we are enduring."

This went on until they arrived at the camp. The old priest had made it.

My mentor said if the younger man had tried to cheer him up with words like, "Come on, you can do it; I know you can," the priest would have died. What suffering needs is compassion. The word compassion means to suffer with someone. The younger man had companioned the priest in his trouble rather than cheering him from a place of strength.

That tree certainly didn't try to cheer my friend. It mirrored her sorrow, her ugly feeling of being alone and abandoned, of being out of balance and out of place, a reject from the warm family light of American Christmas. The tree was my friend's compassionate companion. It's in a box somewhere now, smiling sleepily at the memory of a job well done, a destiny fulfilled, of how it got her through.

LOVE CANT FIX EVERYTHING

I was sitting with a group of Unitarian Universalists talking about the shooting in Knoxville's Tennessee Valley Unitarian Universalist Church when one person said of the shooter, "He just never had any love." Never one to err on the side of gracious silence, I snapped, "He most certainly did have love. I know one of the women who loved him, and she loved him fiercely."

I met him several times, once at a wedding in his back yard, and then at the UU summer camp in Virginia, in 1996. His then-wife, we'll call her Alice, used to attend the Tennessee Valley UU Church. I am a card-carrying liberal, and I think what David (we called him Jabo) did was evil. I don't think he is evil, but the horror he perpetrated on the Tennessee Valley and Westside UU congregations was.

I can't explain a man opening fire during a worship service by saying he wasn't loved. Five women loved him enough to marry him. I used to look forward to UU summer camp so I could sing with

Alice. She loved him fiercely, as I said. They used to talk about how they were soul-twins. He had a family who loved him, too, and he loved them. His mom, his dad, his sister who was a nurse: They loved him. He had good, loyal friends, too. Unfortunately, some of those friends loved drinking and doing drugs with him.

The day I went to my friend Catharine's wedding in Jabo and Alice's back yard was a lovely day. The wedding was fun, with lots of music and laughing, great tattoos on most of the guests, and lots of drinking. I lit the fireworks during the wedding, stone cold sober, of course.

Fast forward ten years of hard drinking and drug use, losing Alice because of his threats to end her life and his, the paranoia that is the hallmark of certain kinds of drug abuse, loss of job after job, and the self-righteous scapegoating of "liberals and gays" encouraged by right-wing blowhards. Add the twist in his heart every time he drove past his ex-wife's church, and you have, I think, the storm that struck Unitarian Universalist congregations of Tennessee and the whole denomination when he walked in to a worship service on a July Sunday morning, drew a shotgun out of a guitar case, and started shooting.

I wish I had a solution to the ills of society. All I have here is a small addition to the conversation among liberals about people who do evil things. Jabo had lots of choices and lots of chances. Maybe it was brain deterioration from the substance abuse, maybe it was the right-wing hate mongering, maybe it was poor impulse control resulting from a chemical imbalance he was born with. Whatever advantages and disadvantages he started with, he participated with his sovereign free will in making himself what he is today. I think this is more respectful of him and his inherent worth than to imply that he couldn't help what he did, that he was on some kind of predestined track to disaster.

Sometimes there is brokenness that just can't be fixed. I'm sorry to say that, but as a minister who worked in the mental health field for twenty years before working full-time at a church, I know that love can't fix everything. Anyone who has been partnered with someone who becomes increasingly isolated in their own reality, who is ill and refuses treatment, or who is in the grip of addiction— anyone who has tried to love someone enough so they get well—knows that. Love cannot always be sweet and outreaching. Sometimes love must be challenging. Sometimes it is more loving to leave someone than to stay. It sends them a powerful message that what they are doing is not OK.

Our churches, likewise, can't help or fix everyone. Living in a covenant community is hard work, and it necessitates our staying on our medication, by which I mean staying in as right a mind as is possible for us. Sometimes a person is not in a place in their life when they have the mental, emotional, and spiritual resources to be part of a covenant community. Covenant communities can be hard on their members, too, because they don't always work the way they say they want to work. You have to have a certain sturdiness to bear that.

I hear folks say that if Jabo had come to a UU church, he would have been helped. My friends, he came to UU summer camp as his argumentative, gun-loving, right wing, liberal-blaming self, and he was argued with, of course. He was derided for being part of the Boy Scout organization and for his right-wing views. He felt disrespected and shunned.

We love to think of ourselves as open-minded, but it's hard for us to be open-minded toward certain people and their views. Maybe it's just me that has a hard time, but I think I'm not alone in this. I argued with him, too. I do affirm the worth and dignity of every person, but I never promised to affirm the worth and dignity of every idea. Some ideas are oppressive and not well thought out. They lead to violence and injustice and really bad behavior. I try to argue with respect and kindness, but it's hard when the person you're talking to acts like a jerk. If I were the Dalai Lama or a UU saint, I would be able to, and I hope that will come in the future, but I am sure not there yet.

I understand wanting to find an explanation for his choice to shoot liberals while a group of their children were performing the show "Annie Jr." If we can explain it, maybe we feel we have some control in the situation, some understanding of ways to prevent it happening to us. Life is dangerous. It is hard and sweet and adventuresome, full and mysterious, and way, way beyond our control. We do what we can.

I lived in Israel for a time, where we all stayed alert to odd behavior, abandoned packages, money lying on the sidewalk that might be wired to explode when you picked it up, people sweating in the cool air, wearing long coats in the summertime. We are all part of the world, even in our churches, and we need some people to be alert so the rest of us can relax our guard when we gather.

I would like to understand all of the reasons why a person would do something evil, but that's not a pressing need for me. I'm not sure we'll ever understand. I think the capability for destruction is within all of us, given certain pressures.

What I do need is to hear stories of courage and kindness. I need the heroes, like Greg, the usher who people say stepped in front of Jabo to protect others and died as a result, like the men who wrestled Jabo to the ground and kept him there. John, one of those men, was playing Daddy Warbucks. He tied Jabo up with the Daddy Warbucks costume's suspenders.

I need to hear about the UUA Trauma Response Ministry Team, which has received nothing but the highest marks for its swift, sensitive, and extraordinarily competent work with the traumatized and grieving people.

I need to hear about the churches of Knoxville, liberal and conservative evangelical churches, whose members pitched in with love and compassion, bringing food and caring for people as they gathered.

I need to hear the story of the hotel clerk who gave the minister of the UU Fellowship of Hendersonville, North Carolina, a discount at his Knoxville hotel when the parking lot attendant saw his Unitarian Universalist license plate holder.

I need to hear about the mayor of Knoxville, who ordered city workers to clean up the crime scene quickly so the congregation could reclaim the sanctuary.

Most of all I love to hear the story of how the cast of "Annie Jr.," after debriefing with the trauma team, came to Rev. Chris Buice, minister of the Tennessee Valley UU Church, fifteen minutes before a worship service on the Monday after the shooting. They asked if they could sing "Tomorrow" again. Friends who were there described the children singing with tears on their cheeks, people with lit candles in their hands, unable to clap at the end, lifting the flames high and stamping their feet, whooping and shouting for those kids, for that song, for the knowledge that tomorrow will come.

THE SECRET OF LIFE AND DEATH
❖

I had a dream about a friend giving me a necklace. She held it out to me and said,

"Here, you can put it around your neck right next to the instructions about living and dying." Looking down, I could see hanging around my neck two decorated cylinders. They reminded me a little of the mezuzahs that a few of my Jewish friends have mounted beside their front doors, little containers for a scripture verse. One cylinder, I supposed, held the instructions for living. The other held the ones for dying.

I mentally fingered those two small cylinders throughout the next morning, thinking about my dream. What would instructions for living and dying look like? Tiny cramped writing, fitting a lifetime of wisdom onto a tiny slip of paper? Would it be a rolled-up scroll? Maybe the tiny scroll would unroll into infinite space and contain everything I needed to know to keep friends, raise my sons, stay healthy, handle money well, do good work, love deeply and long. Maybe it wouldn't be writing at all.

Maybe if I cracked open the cylinder I would hear a voice from inside it whispering into my ear or singing to me. I remembered a friend saying he believed his mom had sent him a message after she died. "Do good. Do no harm. Be present." Maybe those words were written in tiny script inside the cylinder. Maybe it's my favorite Hafiz poem that begins: "We have not come to take prisoners...."

After telling the dream to my friends Charlie and Pat over lunch, my friend Charlie asked, "Well, what do you think was in there?"

"I don't know," I mused. "You know what? I find myself more interested in the instructions for dying than the ones for living."

"Why do you think that is?"

"I've thought about how to live, talked about it, studied it, and I've learned a lot by now. It's going well, I mean, and I think I know how to do it. It's dying I don't know much about. I never really even think about it, except when I hear a scary noise and I'm home alone. Then I just think about how to stay alive, where to hit, what to use as a weapon, that kind of thing."

"What would your instructions for dying be?"

"All I can sense right now is that it might say something like `STAY CALM, ` and that makes sense. I mean, staying calm is usually a good idea, right?"

There ensued a discussion about times in which it might work better not to stay calm.

Pat asked, "Do you think everyone's instructions for living and dying are the same?"

"I don't think so. Could they be? I mean, could the same instructions work for everyone?"

I know we live differently, but do we humans die differently too? As a minister I have sat next to a good number of people as they died. One, struggling to breathe, said "Nobody told me how to do this. How do I die? What do I do?"

"I don't know," I said, holding his hand. "Maybe it's like falling asleep. How do you do that?"

Some people die by just breathing more and more slowly with more and more time between breaths until you realize at some moment that they aren't breathing any more. Some people see their parents or grandparents coming to get them; maybe they talk to the people gathering, people the living can't see. Others see glimpses of another place. My mother, I think, was traveling as she died. We would say "Mama?" She would answer "Just a minute, I'll be right there," and in a moment she would be able to talk to us.

Even though I've been near people who were dying, I don't know what instructions for dying would be. I've known people who called their family on the phone. "Hello? It's me. I'm dying and I just wanted to say goodbye," one lady said calmly to her big sister. Lots of times family gathers around the bedside. I imagine there would be some instructions about forgiving everyone, telling them how wonderful they've been, how much you love them. Maybe you're supposed to use the weight of your last words to tell a loving truth to someone standing there. "Don't marry that woman," you could maybe say. Or "Don't spank that child anymore." Probably the best instructions for dying would be the same as my friends mom sent him for living. "Do good. Do no harm. Be present." And stay calm.

We shrugged and looked down into our salads. I don't think the same instructions would work for everyone. Surely people are born with different weak points, differing strengths, differing tasks. For Pat, loving is easy. For Charlie, paying attention to the physical world is easy. For me, figuring out why people do what they do is easy. Paying attention to the world is hard. Sometimes loving is easy and often it's not. The family I grew up in would have said there was something in the cylinders about giving your life to the Lord. That would have been the instruction both for living and for dying.

If an instruction like "love" were in one of the cylinders, it would feel vague, but I believe I would do my best. "Be kind" would be fine, if I could argue that being kind also includes being challenging and confrontive. What if it doesn't include those things, though? What if challenging and confronting don't do much good in the final accounting? I may need more detailed instructions. Maybe inside one of the cylinders it says something like 'watch." Or 'enjoy." Wouldn't that be a kicker, if the instruction for dying was "enjoy"? Maybe one day there will be a dream where I get to open the cylinders. Then again, if I knew exactly what they said I would probably start rebelling against my instructions. I think my inner wisdom had the right idea just to let me wonder. I may be wondering until I die, trying to remember to stay calm.

BUG ZAPPER

That party at Boyd's place was a clarifying moment for me. I had been in the South, counting the three years spent here as a child and my four years of college, for about the same amount of time I'd spent in the North. I was thinking of myself as assimilated.

Boyd is a good boy. He hunts and fishes, he can find arrowheads anywhere he walks; he just has the eye for them. If the nuclear holocaust comes and I'm still living, I'm going to find Boyd, because he will know what to do.

At this party, we were eating oysters and chicken Boyd had cooked on the grill he made from an underwater mine he found washed up on Sullivan's Island, down near Charleston. It is a huge black metal ball that he cut in half. He welded pipes in there to run propane to the coals, and it works great. On the highway, when he was towing the thing back to Spartanburg, he said, people who recognized what it was gave his old station wagon wide berth. He was pretty sure it wasn't going to explode, but when he got home he found its serial number and called the Navy to make sure it was decommissioned. I'm not completely sure that's the truest of stories, but who knows, with Boyd? It didn't explode, anyway, and now it's a grill.

Night was falling. Supper was winding down. Conversation was flowing in a desultory manner, the way it does when you're sitting around in the South with friends and no one's mad and no one's related. I noticed people pulling lawn chairs over to the shed. "Watch this, Meg," said one of my friends. Boyd took the bug zapper from its hook in the shed and put it down on the dirt floor. We sat in a circle around it. It buzzed often, frying bugs. A murmur rose from the crowd. A line of toads formed, coming out from under the workbench circling around the bug zapper. Six or eight big toads hopped in a circle around the bug zapper, eating the fried bugs, having their own barbeque. I was fascinated. With the toads, with this group of chemists and artists, of schoolteachers and ministers and mechanics, of asbestos removal experts, dancers and college administrators watching the toads, and with my uppermost thought. Which was: "I went to Duke and Princeton Seminary. I am being entertained by toads dancing around a bug zapper. If they could see me now." Then, "Let them see me and snicker. It does not do to get so sophisticated that you narrow the range of things you can find enjoyable. Expand; expand, until at the end of your life you can think almost everything is wonderful. What a wonderful life that will be. "

FAULT LINE

In the living room of my old house there was a ceiling that had been iced. That's what it looked like, anyway, with some kind of spackle swirled over it like the icing that women in magazines from the 1950's used to put on the chocolate cake when company was coming. We called that ceiling "Betty Crocker on acid." Two people had worked on it in tandem. I could tell that because the swirls were thick and exuberant on exactly one half of the ceiling, with waves of spackle frozen in mid-crest. On the other side of a line down the ceiling's middle were more swirls of spackle, only these were uniformly shallower; more conservative.

It's not really noticeable at first glance. You have to be looking at the ceiling with nothing else in mind. I noticed it one Christmas when I was so sick I lay on the sofa in the living room for three days. I lay on that sofa and stared at the ceiling, letting the mild December light wash over me through the sheer curtains. That's when I noticed the disagreement about how thick the swirls should be, how large they should be, how much one should let oneself go in applying the material. I know it wasn't one person who had a change of heart in the middle of the job. In that case the change would have been more gradual, less exactly halfway across.

I don't know if the two spoke to one another as they worked. I am certain they each disapproved of how the other was laying on the spackle. Did they just agree to disagree? Did they let it ride, unspoken? Did they fight over it; each entrenched in one view of the right way to do the ceiling? I wondered whether the two who iced that ceiling were a couple or workers on the same crew. If they were workers, surely there was a supervisor to whom they would have appealed; someone who would have made the call concerning how thick the swirls should be, or someone who would have said, "Let's just wait until the popcorn sprayer is fixed. We don't have to do this today."

I think a supervisor would have chosen the thinner application, which would use less material and cost less. I was pretty sure this was a couple; these were people whose disagreements had a long history, people who knew what the other would say about just about everything. Maybe it wasn't even worth bringing up. He knew how their conversation would go. It would be like talking to a brick wall. He looked at the road ahead and give up right then, made a turn, didn't even go there. She would have thought he was set in his ways; he was so sure he was right, that there was only one way to do things. Why even bother? Why even try? Being right was more important than having a ceiling that made sense.

The I Ching calls this "bringing a lawsuit," and advises against it. A "lawsuit" is when you have decided how someone is, what they are going to do, who they are going to be, so much so that you leave them no room in your mind to change. It's a way of giving up on someone. I have done that before – decided that it is so hard to talk to someone that you don't even begin the conversation. You already know how it's going to go.

When my marriage was ending, I wrote a scene in my novel where a woman was leaving a man. I wrote what she said, and I wrote how he answered her. Sensible at first, then angrier, his need, his accusation, her weariness, her anger, the burnt cinder of her heart, the death of her will to try any longer. When I did leave him, we had that very conversation. A few weeks later, he said, "I read the scene you wrote. I don't think it's right for you to use our real conversation verbatim like that." I told him to go look at the date on that chapter's computer file, that he would see it was written a full year before we had our recent conversation. I find it sad that I knew what he would say, what I would say, every twist and turn of the dialogue. The I Ching said I should have imagined he might respond differently.

I know how to leave someone room to be different from me. Now I need to figure out how to leave someone room to be different from who I think I know them to be. How do I protect myself against being hurt or driven to exhaustion by someone's actions, someone's talking and thinking patterns, and yet still leave them room to move, to change? I don't know. I'm not the only one who doesn't know. That is a comfort. I looked up at that ceiling and saw another couple who didn't know how to engage in the conversation. They left each other alone about it, and lived under a ceiling that was a visible symbol of an invisible division. Given my policy to try to tell the best story about something that can be told within the parameters of the evidence, I imagine them staying together for years, knowing what conversations were worth having and when it was time just to agree to disagree. The two halves of their icing did the job, stayed together, and made a pretty good ceiling. If you didn't look too closely you might say it looked like an anniversary cake baked on an exuberant day.

RODE HARD

Remember the Rorschach inkblot tests that psychologists give? You're supposed to say what the patterns make you think of. The old blots were one color only, but now they are multi-colored. I had a friend who was getting her PhD in psychology. She tested me one day. I was having fun, entertaining myself. "Ooh, that one looks like two teenage girls in the deepest jungle holding hands and dancing around a cooking pot," I said.

"This one -- it's what's left of a hotel room after two aliens have had a fight to the death."

She squinted at me and said 'Bats and butterflies, Meg. If anyone ever gives you this test, just say bats or butterflies. "

Life is like an inkblot. You can tell a lot about another person by how they look at events. Here is what led up to my writing this while I'm standing up because it hurts too much to sit down. I was at a friend's house on Lake Lure with my boys and one of their friends. We were playing in the water. The three teenage boys were diving, yelling, swimming and floating. I was reading. They worked up their courage to jump off the second story of the boathouse, high above the water. Soon they were daring each other to perform twists and spins, to kick soccer balls while in the air. I was reading. I looked up every time a boy plummeted from the roof above me into the water. Once in a while I would dive off the dock and swim around to cool off. Rainstorms were sweeping through the valley that day, so now and then we would get to swim among raindrops, which felt dreamy and poetic.

The boys were having so much fun jumping off the second story of the boathouse; I decided I would do it too. I remember walking up the steps, coming up onto the flat roof, looking down. The water looked far away, gleaming dully, metallic. My younger son said "Oh, Mom, that's not a good idea. You might hurt yourself." His friend said, "Cool! Go! Go!" My oldest said "She's going to do it anyway, just let her go." I jumped. I meant to go in feet first, but something else happened. I hit sitting down. The impact felt like that paddle my first grade teacher used on me once at Mulberry Street Elementary School. I swam back to the dock with all the dignity I could muster. I didn't actually say, "Didn't hurt! " but I was attempting to convey that with my attitude. I eased myself into the lounge chair to read for the rest of the afternoon. It wasn't until the next day that I realized I had really hurt something. It felt like I was sitting on a tennis ball made out of bone. It was the kind of discomfort that builds until you can't think, and your vision narrows, and nothing outside of that feeling can hold your attention.

I've been dealing with it. For the past week or so I have been noticing how much one sits down in the course of a day. I was shifting and grimacing in the hairdresser's chair. His sister asked how I had hurt myself. I told her I felt so good at the lake that I forgot I was in my late forties with a fifteen year old hip replacement and I got brave.

"Not brave, daredevil," she said, shaking her head at me.

"I don't see the difference," I said.

"Mmmmmm-hmmm," said my hairdresser. "That's what I'm talking about."

The doctor I finally went to said "Hey, at least you had fun on the way down."

My chiropractor said, "You let your desire to hold onto your youth override your common sense, eh?"

It's funny how people see it differently. Life, ink blots. Getting older takes some thinking about, and people seem to think about it in a couple of ways. Some people resign themselves to it early. They start talking about being old when they aren't old yet. Other people resist being old with every fiber of their will. Some people admire you when you don't act your age, others shake their heads. I'm trying to figure out where to stand in all of this, how to live gracefully in this body at this age.

A dear friend said, "You're just you and that's the way you do it." Yep, foolish or brave, I use everything I've got pretty hard -- my clothes, my car, my body. I will pretend to learn from this.

NO MORE GOING WITH THE FLOW
❖

We thought it would be fun to go tubing as a family. When I thought of tubing, I pictured us lazily trailing our fingers in the river, soaking up fresh air, dappled sunlight, silky green water.   My first surprise was when I found out that the two Western North Carolina rivers I researched for our expedition don't have water all the time. It's not that sometimes there is rain and sometimes there is drought.   I mean that Duke Energy Company opens the gates on the dam some days and lets water rush into the stream bed. You have to call the tubing place around ten on the day you want to go to find out whether there will be water. You have to be in the river by one because after that the water levels drop and you'll be stuck in the rocks.

We called around ten. There was going to be water. We left plenty of time to get there, but some friends wanted to come, and we needed to stop for suntan lotion. The place was only five miles from the turn-off, but it was a winding five miles where if you pushed over 35 miles an hour you were taking your life in your hands. We ran for the campground office as soon as we got there. The woman behind the counter seemed calm but her husband was making big "hurry up" gestures with his arms and shouting "Come on! Let's go! Let's get in the bus now!" We ran for the bus and he floored it around the road's curves with the six of us and six of another family, grandmother, mama, daddy, grandfather, two little kids, maybe 8 and 9 years old. Screeching to a stop by a rickety railing by some stairs leading down to the river, he ran around the back of the truck and pulled the bungee cord off of twelve big yellow plastic donuts.

"If you make it through this part, you'll have no trouble after this!" he said, a little too cheerfully. "Keep the little ones in front of you, that way if they get in trouble you can be right there." We nodded, and he dropped us into the water. It was rough whitewater sliding over big smooth rocks, which we cleared, and we were all okay on the other side of them. We got ready to relax and go with the flow. The current was swift, and the lightweight kids were quickly swept away out of sight. At the next rapids I got dumped out. The raft was so tightly inflated and the current was so fast that it was hard to get back up on it. With my partner Kiya's help I finally managed, heart beating wildly, sending up thanks for the weights I'd worked with at the gym over the past months, and for her lifeguard training and lifeguard nature. I gave up going with the flow, kicking my feet to get to the middle of the river because the flow kept taking me toward the bank, into eddies under low-hanging trees. That sounds lovely, except the branches were covered with spiders. I don't mind spiders one at a time, but in a spider convocation they get to me.

I alternated between kicking to try to control where I was and telling myself to surrender to the experience. People are always telling me to take it easy, be a feather on the breath of God; they tell me not to try to control things so much. I had the brief thought that if I surrendered, the river would respond from its best self and give me a nice ride. After going with the flow into a submerged tree, caught in branch after branch, having to kick off from it without getting one of my feet stuck, I decided I was through with surrendering. I was going to steer as hard as I could. I had lost sight of Kiya when the river took her around one side of a long island and my son, his girlfriend and me down the other.

The river was very shallow at this point, and rocky. One big smooth rock caught my tube and flipped me out into the water, so I tried to stand up. It should have been easy enough; the water was less than knee deep, but the current kept sweeping my feet out from under me. It ripped the tube out of my hands. Suddenly I remembered a paddler friend saying, "When you lose control, just point your feet downstream and go." So I did. I became a human raft, bouncing and scraping over the rocks, crashing into my son, his friend and my tube under a tree on a shallow beach. We rested a while. Surely it wouldn't be too much farther to the place where we could get out. Finally we caught sight of Kiya downriver. She was shaken. She'd come upon the little girl caught in a sucking swirl of water that was bouncing her tube around amongst some rocks, threatening to upend her. Kiya made her way over to the girl. While freeing her, she herself was picked up by the swirl and jammed headfirst into sharp submerged rocks. It was a pure World Wrestling pile drive from the river. She'd managed to get back on the yellow tube, only to be swept a few moments later into a submerged tree, dumped again, and made to fight through the branches against the strong current to find the surface. It sounded like the river was trying to kill her.

We all made it back to the campground, relieved that everyone in both families was alive, mad at the tubing man for acting like this stretch of the river was no big deal. The whole back of my body from shoulders to ankles was scraped raw and bruised dark purple for a week. Kiya was okay until the second day, when her neck seized up and would not move for several days.

My picture of tubing as a lazy float is in shreds. My trust in the guy at the journey's edge who speaks reassurances is gone. Whatever faith I had in sweet surrender to the Flow is on hiatus. Who says you have to be reverent about the Flow, anyway? Why should I trust it? Do I just surrender to every flow that comes along? I'm not an easy flowing person. Being introduced to a branch full of spiders is going to make me kick. Am I unspiritual? Heck no. You know why? My will and I are part of this flow. My kicking is part of what happened at the river that day. You've got to know when to steer, when to glide, and when to kick like hell to change your situation. Sometimes you've got to say "no" to the flow

As I write this, it's Hanukkah. At my Unitarian Universalist church we're celebrating the miracle where one tiny vial of sacred oil burned for eight days. The Jews had driven the Empire's soldiers out of Jerusalem, and the temple had been cleansed of the desecration, the big lie that had been erected in the holy of holies. The desecration of the temple was supposed to wipe out the Jews' spirit and their culture, but instead it made them angry enough to revolt. The temple had to be consecrated, but most of the holy oil had been polluted by the Empire's soldiers. The one vial of oil lit the lamps for long enough for more sacred oil to be made.

Right now in my congregation we are having a lively conflict that arose when someone wrote in our newsletter that UUs don't believe in miracles. I am very comfortable with conflict. (I'm going to say that till it's true.) The church folks are handling the conflict well. Words of hurt and anger are already evolving into self-revelation, and I think that understanding will come next, then compassion. Everyone has copied me on the email discussion. I thought I would have to jump in more than I have, but they are getting there on their own. That in itself seems miraculous to me!

I don't really care whether the oil really historically verifiably burned for eight days. I absorb faith stories the same way I think and feel about dreams. If the story of Hanukkah were my dream, it would be about being under menacing pressure to give up my truth. It would be saying there was a desecration, a lie, set up in my Holy of Holies.

The idea that I'm busy, pressed, doing useful and important things, that I can't take a detour into an arena in cowgirl boots—that might be a lie. The sense that I'm special, that great things are expected of me, that I have to be more productive, more gracious, more present than other people, that I mustn't rest as much, have as much fun, or live my life simply to enjoy it—that might be a lie. I may need to toss out the fuel I've been running on, a sense of grinding obligation that I've been trying to live up to. That fuel has my lamp sputtering and stinking this time of year.

At the concert a little miracle happened to me. My lamp was re-lit by what Harry did, encouraging my creativity, wanting me to have a little treat. Who knows how long that little vial of oil will burn?

THE WIND THE WAY IT IS
❖

I was exhausted and off balance in the storm of sorrow, loss, pride, love and confusion that hit me when my younger son moved out of the house to go to college. Two of my best friends and I managed to wrestle our schedules to the ground and get away for two whole days to a mountain house in Blowing Rock, North Carolina. Susan's family had spent every summer since she was a little girl. Ellen and I took in the stone foundation, the white wood siding, the green trim, the steep lawn with its dark enormous rhododendron bushes. Susan's siblings, all now in their sixties, still use the house, fussing good naturedly about how much to spiff it up, how tacky or how convenient it would be to update the kitchen and the bathrooms, whose family photos should be placed most prominently on the tables and the mantelpiece. Should everyone pay for the updates or only the siblings who are in favor of them? Should the ones who use the house most pay the most or should the ones with the most money pay the most?

Susan hadn't been up to the house in several years. An elderly man with a mower appeared around the corner of the house. She recognized him as the same man who had kept the yard since she was a girl. Manners dictated that before we could begin unloading the car, they had to have a little chat to get caught up with one another's lives. He was doing fine, but his wife was in poor health. Susan's oldest sister's grandbaby had been up for a visit at Christmas time. Hard to believe. He remembered that sister at sixteen in pedal pushers and red lipstick. That couldn't have been fifty years ago, but here it was. Ellen and I leaned against the car nodding and smiling.

After we lugged our suitcases up the stone steps, onto the wide porch, into the living room and up to the bedrooms, I chose a room with corner windows and a green view of the trees surrounding the house. A small black box was resting on the uneven floor, plugged into a wall outlet. All I could guess from the name printed on the box was that it was a gizmo that kept mice away with sound waves. Sonic-mouse-away or something like that is what they called it. I sat on the bed and kept my feet off the floor.

There was no food in the house, so that evening we drove down the hill into town. A grocery store was open, a tiny market with a deli. Half the store was taken up with maps and souvenirs depicting the Chickasaw legend of Blowing Rock. An Indian brave, torn between the woman he loved and his duty to the tribe, threw himself off an outcropping of rock on a windblown mountainside. His beloved, a beautiful maiden, prayed and pleaded with the winds until they reversed themselves, blowing backwards and upward, returning her love to her side. To this day, honoring their love, the winds blow up instead of down the mountain it that one place. Clutching a drinking glass with a picture of the maiden on it, I bought cheese, crackers, bread and wine for supper. It has been one of my dreams to make a five-course meal with each course a different kind of cheese. My dream came true that night. We drank wine and laughed and talked. We decorated the rooms with orange bittersweet we'd picked while walking the neighborhood that afternoon. We rocked on the porch in the dark, rearranged the family pictures on the mantel to return the ones of Susan's children to the front row, and then read ourselves to sleep. I woke up feeling like my life might go on all right.

A new study out of UCLA says that the old theory that people have a "fight-or-flight" response to stress was based on studies done mostly with male subjects. Apparently the female brain under stress releases a whole different cascade of chemicals that urge the female to "tend-and-befriend" in addition to fighting or flighting---uh – fleeing. Reading that, I remembered one time while watching a scary movie I had an almost irresistible urge to go get my children and have them right next to me. Now I know that it was my female chemistry buffering the fight or flight response, encouraging me to tend to my children and gather with friends. When we obey the urge do this tending and befriending, calming chemicals are released.

Life brings scary changes. Things go over the cliff. Your roles, your health, certainties, routines, ways of being in the world that you took for granted. You plead with the winds to return them to you. You pray. You cry. In my life the winds have not reversed themselves to bring back youth or familiar routines. I don't know whether I would really want them to.

Some of what I've lost has been replaced. Mothering my now adult sons is a fresh adventure. They are people I'm proud to know, men I'm glad the world has in it. They love amazing two amazing women, and I'm glad to have them in my life. Through it all, these friends and I have held one another up. If we could be the wind we would restore all losses: a husband's hearing, spreading arthritis; we would keep all children and grandchildren healthy and untroubled.

We can't be the wind. What we can do is sit together and drink a little wine, break bread and eat some cheese, dangling our feet off the edge of this cliff that we are all on, always, and hold on as long as we can.

A LITTLE CHANGE

❖

I was checking out at the Family Dollar store, six cents short at the register. Usually if you're just a penny shy of what you need they will say, "Don't worry about it." Six cents, though, that's more than a "don't worry about it" amount. Digging through my pockets for the rest and coming up empty, I turned to apologize to the man behind me for holding up the line. He looked tired; his mahogany skin, his clothes and his work boots were all filmed grey with cement dust. He hadn't shaved in several days. His sweatshirt had a couple of holes in it where his t-shirt showed through.

"Sorry," I said.

"What you need?" he asked.

"Six cents," the clerk and I said together. Then she said, "Listen, it's okay."

At the same time he said, "I got you."

"Thanks," I said to the clerk and to the man at the same time.

"It's no problem," he said.

If I were to stop telling it here, this could make a good simple story. If I were not over-responsible, a first-born, a Virgo, raised with Scots Protestant values, it could have ended like that. Instead, what happened next was that I went out to my car and rooted through the change compartment, found six pennies, went back in, and put them on the counter. "Here you go," I said, turned around and walked back out.

"I could a got you," he said, to my back.

I could not have driven out of that parking lot having taken anything from those two people. I didn't want them watching my taillights, musing about how a middle class white woman took six cents off them without looking back. I think now that it might have felt more respectful to accept the gift with thanks.

I have been chewing over this, asking myself questions about it. Would I have accepted six cents from a white-skinned man standing in the line behind me? A white-skinned woman? A dark-skinned woman? Would I have taken six cents from a friend? "Yes" to that last one. "No" to everyone else. Never. I didn't realize I was so stiff-necked.

What would it have hurt to owe another person a little, walking out of that store? Am I pretending that I'm self-sufficient in this world? It's an illusion some wealthier people can preserve for a little while, at least. Would I have accepted an offer of help carrying something heavy to my car? Yes. He looked rich in physical strength, more than I was. I would have gladly accepted help from his wealth, but not from an area in which I assumed he was poorer than I. Allowing someone to help me out of their weaker place is too hard. It would be like me offering to carry something for him to his car. What a tangled mess all of this is.

I tell people that it is good to learn to accept help as well as to help. It's good practice for times of sickness or when we are less physically able at certain times. If we are hard to help, our helpers not only have to help us, they have to endure our grumpiness and outrage at needing help, our snappishness and embarrassment. It's easier for most of us to be the helper. I wouldn't think anything of giving someone six cents in line, even a dollar or two. I'm hoping that after a few more spiritual growth cycles I can be the kind of person who could accept six cents from another human on the planet who could feel a little good about helping somebody else at the end of a long day laying concrete. It would be just a little change, and what's so hard about that?

A FLAT TIRE AND A BEATING HEART

It started with a flat tire. Well, it actually started a couple of days before that. Right after Christmas we walked for hours around Manhattan in the freezing air: Chelsea, the Village, the Bowery. Now and then we stopped to get warm, once in a coffee shop and once at a poetry marathon. All that frigid air was shocking to my Carolina lungs, so I was having a little trouble with what felt like allergies. I took a couple of different medications and went to bed.

In the middle of the night I woke up with my heart banging against my breastbone faster than I'd known it could go. "Too much allergy medication," I thought, and fell back asleep thinking it would be better in the morning. It was, but I still felt weak and strange. On the schedule was an engagement to preach for a congregation on Long Island. I like to preach so much that I would do it with one foot in a fire, so I had fun talking and singing with the people that morning. When I was through I felt faint and had to sit down.

Several people came in from the parking lot in back of the church to say that there was a white car out there with a flat tire. It was the Chevrolet we'd rented in Newark. A dapper man with a red-gold mustache, blue eyes, and a lovely suit held both my hands and told me he would be delighted to change the tire for us. He went out with Kiya to get started.

When I got out there he (we'll call him Craig) was kneeling on the ground placing the jack under the car. A very tall young woman (we'll call her Lou) was giving him instructions on where to put it. Another tall woman, a friend of Lou's, was standing with us. "You know a lot about this," I said to Lou.

"Back in Tennessee I got my mechanic's certification," she said. "It was hard there because no one understood what I was going through, but finding these friends and this church just saved my life."

I realized she was talking about a life back home where people would have looked at her and seen a man. The other woman standing with us was going through that same transformation. The four of us stood and watched Craig change the tire after getting him a car mat to kneel on so he wouldn't scuff up his trousers. He was glowing, changing that tire, while we admired his efforts.

A woman came out of the church. Seeing us standing there, she called out to me, "Oh, you talk a good game about women's empowerment"—that's not at all what I had talked about, but people hear what they will hear—"and there you are, four women watching one man change a tire." The five of us glanced at her and smiled. What she was actually looking at was more complicated than one could gracefully explain. Kiya started laughing a little. She was still smiling when we got in the car, having treated the very happy Craig to a round of applause.

"What are you smiling about?" I asked her.

"Here is what you don't know," she said. "Craig told me it had always been one of his fantasies to change a tire heroically in front of a crowd of appreciative women. We were making his fantasy come true."

"Fun," I said.

I was also laughing about what that woman said about four women watching one man change a tire."

"Yeah?"

"She didn't know what she was seeing, all the way."

"No."

"What she also didn't know is that Craig told me he used to be a woman."

Feeling weaker and weaker as the day went on, I got on the plane to come home. By the time we landed, I was a flat tire. We went straight from the airport to the doctor, to the emergency room, to the Heart Center of the hospital.

Apparently the weakness was caused by my heart racing like a wild horse, beating to its very own rhythm. Samba, rumba, 5/4, 2/4, then 9/8 in the next measure. For eight days they tried to get the wild horse to slow down, and did every heart test I'd ever heard of. The good news was that my heart was healthy, with no build-ups and no blockages. After they sent me home, my heartbeat went back to normal.

An adventure like that is one way to wake up to the beauty of the day. I'm in love with my heartbeat now, and I feel the heartbeat in people who are around me. The planet looks to me these days like billions of hearts beating, flashing sparks of light, a cacophony of drums, small and large, fast and slow, all holding one basic rhythm. A beating heart is something we all have in common. A heartbeat is one thing you want to do like everyone else. What surrounds the heartbeat, though, that's where we take in the feast of wild variation.

That Lou and Craig have found their right rhythm gives me courage. It feels like beauty and magic to have met them when I was out of my own rhythm. I'm on the road again, friends. Thanks.

ONE OF THOSE ANGRY WOMEN
❖

When I heard that Mary Daly had died, I wrote on my Facebook page that she had changed my life. That ferocious theologian was among those writers responsible for the unraveling of my Presbyterian Christianity. I find myself hesitating to write about her, knowing that it means approaching the thick tangle of culture, gender, anger, and God. In that place, scorpions patrol and guard, tails lifted and ready to strike at a misstep in thought, feeling, or choice of words. As the witches say, "Where there's fear there's power," so here I go.

I was at Princeton Seminary when The Church and the Second Sex and Beyond God the Father first tugged with insistent fingers on one or two threads of the theology I had wrapped around me like a lumpy and uncomfortable sweater. The two threads were the way women were treated and the language that was used for speaking about God. Daly was a professor at Boston College with one doctorate in Theology and one in English, and the school had attempted to fire her after her first book was published. The all-male student body rose in support of her and she'd been given tenure. Her thinking was clear, and I would read her insights and her questions and marvel that I'd never seen things that way before, obvious as they now were. "Hmm," it made me think. "Look at this: If we speak of God as Father and King, it's as if we are saying God is male. If our religion speaks of God as male, then maleness is closer to God-ness than femaleness is."

I began wondering if that's why men were in charge of so much of the world. Maybe that's why, when I want to look up a married woman friend in the phone book, I have to know her husband's name. Maybe that's why I can pass a house with toys in the yard and two cars in the driveway, but can only see the name "Steven Bobo" on the mailbox. Maybe that's why the Senate was mostly men, there isn't a national holiday named after a woman, and there hasn't of this writing ever been a female U.S. president.

I got mad. My mother worried. "Oh, Meggie," she said, "don't become one of those angry women." Too late, Ma. I had enough of the warrior in my nature to want to take it all on, point it out, make it right. Gyn/Ecology: The Metaethics of Radical

Feminism, Daly's 1978 book, showed me the war against women and children that has been waged for centuries using the threat of violence to control every situation. Women become afraid of men's violence, so they need a protector and they do what that protector says. Much later, in the mid-'90s, it happened twice that, when my husband and I would mention that I was taking karate, a man would instantly say, "Guess you won't be able to tell her what to do anymore."

Daly's books were a-mazing, in that she helped me see the maze that was patriarchy, and helped me attempt to step out of it. She played with the language that way, and wrote about deviant/defiant women doing metaphoric/metamorphic work.

After seminary, with the two threads of my uncomfortable sweater dangling, the following years' experiences tugged and tugged, until little by little my Presbyterian Christianity came completely apart and lay in an awkward pile at my feet.

Then came another kind of turning point. In my late twenties I was at a party with my then-husband where the women all congregated in the kitchen and talked about children and diets and the men congregated in the living room to watch the game. Not fitting in either place, even though I was friends with all of the people, I drifted back and forth between the two groups. Leaning against the opening to the living room, I called out, teasing, to the guy holding the remote, "There's the man holding the remote, in control of the whole world." I'll never forget the look on his face as he turned toward me. It was open, puzzled, bewildered, and a little sad. It was clear that he didn't feel in control of much.

As a couple's counselor for many years, I heard countless women say they felt controlled by their partners. Countless men told me they felt controlled by their partners. As more same-sex couples came to me, many of them felt controlled by their partner. "If everyone is feeling controlled," I thought, "who is doing all the controlling?" Maybe the culture controls everybody who doesn't struggle to wake up. Maybe it's patriarchy, maybe it's the archetypes. Maybe it's what people name the devil. My anger dissipated. The culprit had become more complicated.

In those years, Mary Daly was spiraling into a place where I couldn't follow her. She was making up her own language, banning males from her classes, spewing venom that shocked me with its acid bite. I couldn't go there with her. She scared me, making me wonder if her anger had run so hot that she'd become isolated in her own reality. Maybe she'd been on the front lines of the fight so long that she was like a traumatized soldier, lashing out with maximum force at times where it didn't feel to me to be warranted. Who can say? I withdrew from her in the same way that everyone avoided the angry-looking madman stomping down the street the other day in New York City yelling, "Face the facts! Face the facts! Face the facts! Face. The. Facts!"

I raised two sons, and began to be a warrior on their behalf as well. Why do men die ten years earlier than women? Why is it okay to send young men to war? Why do men have to wear neckties? Listen to the word. Neck. Ties. Daly would have had a hey-day with that, if she'd turned her mind in that direction. We would say about high heels, "They just want women not to be able to run away," but you could say about neckties, "They just want to have a way to hang men quickly if they don't do right." Why was it okay for the girls in my sons' elementary and middle-school classes to male-bash hurtfully, often with the participation of the teacher? Why are so many husbands on TV commercials portrayed as being so stupid? If women were portrayed that way we would get mad.

I worried for my sons that having male God-language is as bad for men as war. Maybe because the culture speaks of God as male, men feel they have to be omnipotent, omniscient, never needing to ask for directions or say, "Gee, I don't know." Maybe they feel like they should be able to control everything and they feel like failures when they can't do it.

Daly was right. The way things are isn't good for anyone, and it's not good for the planet. I don't think men win here. I don't know who to blame for this situation. I believe most of us are blind to it. Most of us participate in perpetuating it. I'm not sure how to stop. I do what I can. I am not sorry that I used to be "one of those angry women." There were good reasons to be angry.

There are still good reasons to be angry. I just don't know where to point my anger. Can anger help fuel a change or do we have to let go of anger and fuel change with compassion and love instead? I don't know. I'm pretty good at both. In every movement for cultural change there are internal disagreements about those who might be "making us look bad," those who are "setting us back," or "going too far." Daly was the one who stalked the edge, who held that territory so the rest of us could be sweetly reasonable, or at least less terrifyingly demanding. I'm grateful to her for that, and for making me look at my faith and start to face the facts.

BONFIRE OF THE RECLINERS

❖

I spent years married to a man who watched TV. For most of seventeen years I saw the side of his face. We had many conversations with little eye contact. I blame the chair. It was so comfortable, so accommodating. It made no demands, with its plain green background and tiny cream dots, the little rip along the piping under his right knee. He could sit there after supper and control the world with the remote.

Over the years, I got mad. It's funny -- sometimes I don't know I'm mad; it feels like boredom or anxiety. Then it crossed my mind one evening that I would like to bash the TV to pieces with a log from the fireplace. It occurred to me then that I might be feeling angry. I thought I might put a tiny ad in the newspaper that would read something like this: "Women: Meet at 10 Friday night on the town square. Bring the TV, your husband's chair and the remote for a huge bonfire." I imagined a traffic jam of women in trucks and SUVs with recliners loaded up, upholstered in leatherette, vinyl, sweet little country prints, plaids, that nappy blue material that covered most chairs in the 80's, and forest green from the '90's. We would help one another unload, tossing the chairs with their greasy arms and sprung seats into a pile. I would delegate the task of dousing the things with lighter fluid to my second-in-command, but I would keep the pleasure of lighting up the bonfire for myself. I imagined the whoosh and roar of the flames leaping into the night sky. I could almost hear the collective "ahhhhhhhhhh" that would sigh from the assembled women as the recliners that had enslaved our husbands' souls were incinerated. Now maybe there would be hope of conversation that included eye contact. We would toss the remote controls on the pile when the flames were strong. Maybe we wouldn't burn the TVs. Maybe we would.

My husband kept peacefully watching TV in his recliner with the remote. He had no idea that I was furious. That is my fault. I just refined my fantasy of the Bonfire of the Recliners, adding chainsaws. We would slice the chairs up before we burned them. That would make a great angry noise and the destruction would be prolonged.

What do you do when you find out that you are deeply, madly – uh – mad about something? I finally mentioned it to my spouse. He said "uh-huh." I mentioned it again and he got mad. What happens then? Do you say, "This is serious enough that I'm thinking of leaving you?" That comes across as an ultimatum when actually it's just information. In all my years of experience as a couple's counselor, I've never seen someone truly believe how serious the situation has become until they are left. Then, for six months, they become the person the one who left them always wanted.

I know it's not just men who lose their souls to the recliner and the remote. I have seen it happen to women too. People lose their souls to so many things; anyone could make a list. How hard do you push a partner to change? What right do you have to ask for changes at all? What changes will they ask of you in return? What if they cannot change? What if the bitter bottom line is that they would rather have the recliner than the relationship? Do you really want to find that out? Is it the comfort of the thing that destroys? Is it the ease? I don't think comfort is dangerous in itself. I like comfort. Maybe it's the TV. It can be educational, sure, but what regular person can compete with an entertainment machine with writers, sports teams, special effects, and a multi-billion dollar budget? TV erases the subtleties, the nuances of human communication. Everything is big and colorful and obvious. TV also avoids the complexities of touch. It never tries to touch you. You don't have to decide whether you trust it, whether you like it. It doesn't need you. It only gives and makes no obvious demands. Just your attention and your time, two things that mean love when you give them to another human being. What do they mean to the TV?

Yeah, I think a bonfire is a good idea.

MOTHER NATURE

A few years ago I was preaching a sermon about depression, and I mentioned that adults who were neglected as children have a high incidence of depression. Scientists experimented on poor little rat babies, taking them from their poor little rat mamas for a couple of days at a time, then finding chemicals in their spinal fluid when they grew up that were different from the chemicals in other rats. I just happened to mention that I felt sorry for the little rat babies, having to be experimented on, and then I mentioned that I wished instead that they had done the experiments on little possum babies, since there is a possum family that takes turns waking me up at midnight and then again five am going out and coming in to their apartment which they have moved into under my house. I am mad at all possums these days because they don't care at all if I sleep well.

Three days after I said that I got an email from a woman in my church who is much kinder and more compassionate than I. She said she wished I would find it in my heart to express more compassion toward the little possum babies. She added that this message wasn't really even from her, it was from Her -- Mother Nature.

Usually, when I get a note like that I try to search in it for criticism that might be helpful to me and then shrug the rest off. That's a lie. I get mad and defensive first, vow revenge and compose a long letter of self-justification. THEN I calm down, look for what might be useful, delete all the stinky things I wrote and thought, and try to shrug the rest off.

Her letter got me thinking about Mother Nature and the possum babies. The nature-worshippers I know roll their eyes when people tell them what a sweet and nurturing deity the Mother must be, how tender it must be to worship her. Many of them have had actual experience with nature, you know, like outdoors in the winter. In the woods in the summer. Living in a body. Ticks, roaches, frostbite, mosquitoes, cancer.

I decided not to answer this gentle letter of suggestion for my spiritual development, but it was not to be that easy to behave myself. In a crowd at the Spring Home Show at the downtown auditorium there she was by a display of wooden shutters.

"Did you get my note?" she asked, sweetly.

"Yes I did, thank you." I said. Not equally sweetly, but almost.

"I just felt it was something you would want to think about," she said. "It wasn't even a message from me, it was from Her." OK. I have trouble with people speaking for God. Always have. Whenever someone says they have a message for me from the Spirit, it puts my back up. I don't care whether people call God him or Her, Allah, Yemayah or Nana, I have trouble with messages delivered to me through people who want to improve me. If I were more wise, my father used to say, I would love reproof. Maybe I will get there someday. "The message was from Her?" I asked. "Okay. I have a message for you to give back to Mother Nature from me." The woman started to protest. I raised my hand. "Oh, no, please let me finish. If you want to talk about caring for baby possums, you tell Her I care much more than she apparently does, because, even with my feelings about them I have not killed one. Yet. She on the other hand, presides over the deaths of thousands of babies, not only possums but animals of every kind. And she gives no evidence of caring. I mean, you and I could freeze to death in the woods and the breeze would still whisper sweetly in the trees, the moon would still hang silver in the branches, the stars would look on undimmed as our little light went out. When it comes to callousness I've got NOTHING on Her. I can't hold a candle for her to see by!"

A little part of me was watching and saying "Meggie, you are ranting. This woman has taken three steps backward. She does not deserve this." But I couldn't stop.

I used to have a friend who would chide me for pulling living pansies out of my garden when they had grown leggy and wild. I should let nature take its course, she said. Listen, I would tell her. If I were

ROUGH MAGIC

❖

I remember "Boo at the UU." Cool night, velvet dark. Pushing your way through spider webs to get through the front door of the church, you're greeted by comfortingly scary witches and pirates, wizards, cats, and monsters of all shapes and sizes. The big room is filled with fishing games, a cakewalk, and a gigantic spinner where you take your chances on gains or losses, and the basement becomes the "Tunnel of Terror." I have no idea what is down there because just the name gives me the heebie-jeebies. The psychic surgery room, the fortuneteller, and spells and potions are down the hall. Most years I was the fortuneteller, because my Aunt Ruth, the Episcopal priest-psychiatrist, taught me when I was a teenager to read palms and tarot cards.

One year, though, I was put in charge of the spells and potions. I gathered my materials: Amazon rain water, rainbow juice, and liquid sunlight (herbal teas in various colors); wizard spit (honey water); dragon's blood (V8 juice); bat droppings (tiny chocolate chips); lizard tongues (broken flat pieces of pink gum); eyes of newt (sprinkles); vampire blood (chocolate syrup); alchemist's gold (caramel syrup); and various shades of powdered Jell-O and the Pop Rocks that would make a potion bubble and fizz. I was dressed up, all my materials were laid out, I had helpers dressed as wizards, and we were ready. The doors opened and parents and kids came in asking for potions.

"What do you want it for?" I asked. Usually it took them a long time to think of an answer. I wondered why someone would come in to ask for a potion when they didn't know what they wanted it for. Did they simply crave a passing experience, a sweet drink? This was magic we were talking about. It should be taken seriously.

They rose to the occasion.

"I want to run fast," one said.

"Done! You need some confidence, some persistence for practice." I was adding visible and invisible ingredients to a liquid sunlight tea as I spoke. After giving it a final stir with a tiny wand (coffee stirrer), I handed it to one of the wizards who muttered over it for a moment, then delivered it with a flourish to the child.

"I want to be a fairy princess!" Eye of newt, bat drops, alchemist's gold, and fizzy Pop Rocks in wizard spit. "Eeeeeuw!" she said, but drank it up.

A dad said, "I want courage." Well, what would you have done? Dragon's blood with Jell-O and Pop Rocks. It was awful looking. He drank it down. I think he already had courage.

People complained about how awful some of the potions tasted. "What do you want?" I asked, with what I hoped was charm. "Cheap grace? Pretty magic? Magic is rough! Change is hard. If you want something badly enough you may have to do something scary, drink something yucky. Sometimes you get liquid sunlight with sprinkles, but other times it's V8 with blue Jell-O and Pop Rocks."

What happened next was that I was never asked to be potions mistress again. The next year all the potions tasted good and people didn't even have to pony up with what they wanted to have happen in their lives.

This makes me think of the people who describe Mother Nature as sweet and nurturing, taking care of all the little creatures with a warm and cinnamon-scented hand, or those people who say they just knew there had to be a God when they saw the dolphins swimming at sunset. I don't know how ignoring the tough side of nature will help a person through the things church is supposed to help with, or how a dolphins-swimming-at-sunset faith will sustain a person through the rough changes that get slung into his or her life like ninja throwing-stars.

Maybe I went too far with the V8 and Pop Rocks. Usually I'm a very nice minister, but I wouldn't be doing my job if I pretended that our faith wasn't demanding, that the right relationship was easy, or that facing change is a pleasant walk on the beach. Growing asks a lot of us. It takes courage, determination, spiritual practice, strong partnership, and the knowledge that life can be difficult even when you're doing exactly the right thing. Various potions have helped along the way: love mixed with patience, effort, longing, and peace. Liquid sunlight, green Jell-O, lizard tongue, and wizard spit.

Bottoms up.

FIELD TRIP
❖

The school kids in the back of the Rambler station wagon felt Mama downshift to give the engine more power up the steep curve. It threw us forward a little, and jostled us against each other. We were on a Revolutionary War field trip. Three of us were not in the back seat; we were in the WAY back of the station wagon. I fell against my best friend Pam, and she fell against Clifford Scoggins, which was a scream.

Mama was teaching fifth grade that year. I was in fourth grade. My sister was only in second, so she couldn't go. Clifford was in Mama's class, even though he was every bit of fourteen years old. He had been held back several times at Mulberry Elementary School in Statesville, North Carolina. This was his second year in Mama's class. She said his family fed their children an RC Cola and a Moon Pie for breakfast. She said his dad was a sorry cuss, and that was about the worst thing she ever said about somebody. Mama told good stories, kind of nice and kind of mean at the same time. I'm not sure how she did that, but we laughed all the time at the dinner table.

Even though I was only in fourth grade, in Miss Foster's class, Mama had said I could come on the fifth grade field trip and I could bring Pam. We were driving up into the mountains, onto the Blue Ridge Parkway. All the teachers were driving, and some parents were driving too. We waved at the kids in the car behind us and made faces for a while.

Mama played the radio for us, even though probably some of the class parents would fuss because it was devil music. Top 40. It was 1964. Pam could sing "I Wanna Hold Your Hand," and she sounded EXACTLY like the Beatles on the radio. The Beatles were new. Their music shone like candy. It was worldly, foreign but somehow familiar. It was almost like I was remembering the words and the tunes when they sang them, even though I had never heard them before, like there was a place in that music for me if I could figure out how to get in. That spring I wasn't in yet, but it felt like it was right around the corner. Pam was in, yeah, definitely, she was there. Pam and I were singing, "And when I touch you I feel happy inside. It's such a feeling that my love, I can't hide..." It made my heart feel all opened up and smiling.

Clifford looked at her sideways, squinting one eye, smiling crookedly with his lips together. He was way too cool to sing, but he could express appreciation without risking being one of us little kids. One strand of his sandy hair had worked loose of the hair cream, and it curved over his pale freckly forehead. Pam had red hair, and she wasn't smiling while she sang because it was real important to her to remember each and every word just right. her British accent was perfect, I thought. We used to ride horses together out at her house and sing and talk about who we were going to be when we grew up and we'd play redcoat spies and she was a double agent against the British because she could talk like they did. I was George Washington.

When we got out of the cars to look at some old log cabins up on the Blue Ridge Parkway, Mama and the other teacher talked to us about how the people lived, told us we should imagine living in those cabins, having to hunt and fish for food, carry water from the stream, keep the fire going all winter long like they did in Little House on the Prairie. They talked about the Cherokee and the battles fought against the British who didn't want us to have our freedom. Pam and I were riding the horses in our

MAGIC BUS

❖

"When you get to Istanbul," my dad said, "stay in a four-star hotel at least. Try to find some other American girls to go places with." I was twenty, I had been living in Israel for six months, and I didn't pay that much attention to his instructions. On the plane from Tel Aviv to Turkey, I met a young woman from New Zealand, and we decided to hang around together. At the airport we stood in line to get a few of our traveler's checks changed into Turkish Lire. When we got to the window where we would conduct our business, the man shoved the Lire bills at us and muttered under his breath, "Don't say anything to anybody."

"Excuse me?" I wasn't sure if I heard him right.

'Nothing," he looked annoyed.

My friend and I looked at one another. It sounded like something from the Maltese Falcon.
Once on the sidewalk in front of the airport terminal, we headed for a bus whose destination sign read "Istanbul." A cheerful man about our age

walked backward in front of us indicating his car, saying he would give us a ride. "No we're going to take the bus," we said, indicating the bus twenty paces away.

"Is no bus," he said with a shrug.

Even though we didn't talk about them on the bus, those two interactions left both of us a little shaken. I didn't have money for a fancy hotel, I told myself, knowing I was ignoring my father's recommendation even though I was beginning to think he may have had his reasons. Plus, who wanted to be around that many Americans, anyway? We finally found a youth hostel with a couple of free beds. settled into our big four-bunk room with a view of the city. The young woman in the top bunk across the room was nursing a streaming cold, and her friend on the bottom bunk was covered with sores. Something she had picked up in Afghanistan

The Bogart movie feeling came again in the Grand Bazaar. A magnificent warren of curving alleys and covered walkways lined with shops of every description, the place is a visual feast with carpets piled high, brass boxes and pitchers, blown glass, jewelry, spices and food markets. The smells are even better: cardamom, coffee, turmeric and cinnamon. People crowd through the narrow passageways, bumping shoulders with strangers, attempting conversation above the shouts of the shopkeepers calling out offering special prices just for you. I was trying to find my way out of the bazaar toward St. Sophia's, where my traveling buddy and I were to meet up. I asked directions from one shopkeeper and he pointed me down an alley and told me to take a right when I got to the end. After that, whenever I passed ten or eleven shops, a young boy, about nine years old, would dart out in front of me and give me directions for the next turn. Always a different little boy. I don't know where they came from or how they were tracking me, but they got me through the maze and to the church on time.

After a few days of soaking up Istanbul, it was time to leave for Athens. My friend walked me to the bus station that morning. Word at the youth hostel was that any bus to Athens was a twenty-hour ride, and that any bus was okay EXCEPT the "Magic Bus."

"NO Magic Bus," is what everyone said.

I got to the ticket window. "One, to Athens," I said. He told me the price and said the once-a day bus was on time. "No Magic Bus." I said adamantly. He shook his head just as adamantly.

"No, no Magic Bus," he repeated. Satisfied, my friend and I waited on the sidewalk. Ten minutes later, when the bus appeared, it was painted in psychedelic swirls, and across the front glowing letters read: "Magic Bus." Faced with the choice of boarding or waiting another day for the possibility that it would be a different bus, I climbed the steps and took one of the lasts seats available.

Half of the passengers were tiny young women, a dance troupe from Sri Lanka. Three or four of them were traveling with pocket toy poodles. Amongst the noise of yapping and giggling, we took off. Ten hours later, at the Greek border, the soldiers saw the dancing girls on the bus and decided we all had to disembark while they went through our luggage. The girls teetered around on platform sandals and flirted with the guards, whose mood changed from grim and hostile to expansive and jovial. They gave the contents of the girls' suitcases fascinated attention and barely glanced at the less lacy items belonging to the rest of us.

Finally we got going again, along about dark. We dozed. In the middle of the night the bus driver braked to a stop in the road with nothing but fields on either side. "I'll be back," he murmured to those of us who had woken up to see what was happening. He was gone for over an hour, walking off into the darkness carrying a suitcase. When he returned the suitcase was gone. He slid behind the wheel without comment, cranked the engine, and drove the rest of the way to Athens while I, for one, slept a troubled sleep. What would have happened if the soldiers had seen inside that suitcase? What would have happened without the giggling dance girls and their yapping poodles? What would a more normal bus ride have been like? Was I unlucky to have gone to the station on Magic Bus day, or lucky to have had a mildly Bogartian adventure from which I emerged unscathed? I have decided (since I have the choice) to feel lucky and grateful. Do I now decide to take the advice I receive concerning how to have a safer, though perhaps less eventful life? Sometimes I do.

"Magic Happens," the bumper sticker says, and sometimes the Magic Bus happens. May the Sri Lankan dancing girl angels surround you and take you on through.

CUSSING

❖

This love of cussing -- I guess my oldest child got it from me. For most of my life I have tried to speak in pleasant words, well-grounded words. Then I started hanging out with a couple of cussing people. I'm not going to name names, but I'm blaming this squarely on them. I mean, I'm in favor of taking responsibility for my own character defects, but only when I'm forced to do it.

When this child was three and a half, we started toilet training. I thought and thought about a way to make it more appealing to him to sit there in the bathroom waiting for something to happen. One day when I was scolding him about using dirty words, you know, three year old dirty words, like "poo-poo" and "pee-pee" and "bottom," I had an inspiration. Kneeling down to get to eye level, I held his hands in mine and said, "Honey, those are words you can only use when you are sitting on the potty. In fact, when you are sitting on the potty, you may say them as much as you want, or you could even make up a song entirely from potty words." His eyes lit up. From there on out, the training went like a dream. We would sit together, I on the edge of the tub, he on the throne, and we would sing "Pee-pee pee-pee, poo-poo bottom," and we would laugh uproariously. Neither of us could believe we were getting away with what we were getting away with.

Later on, when he was eleven, he said something was crap. Now, in Philadelphia, I grew up not knowing that was a bad word. My dad, who never cussed in my presence, (except once when I was fifteen, but that's another story) said things were crap all the time. Again, struck by a dubious inspiration, I said, "You're not allowed to say `crap` until you're twelve." People in my generation, the baby boomers, don't seem to want to grow up because the grown-ups forgot to make being grown up look appealing. They said things like "enjoy this while you can, because when you grow up you'll have to worry about paying bills and taxes and being responsible." I figured I needed to make getting older have some appeal. In the spirit of that moment, I thought cussing was something that would make it feel cool to reach twelve, maybe balance out my rule that kids had to start doing their own laundry at twelve as well. On his twelfth birthday, this came back to haunt me. "I'm happy as crap to be twelve," he crowed, "get away from me!" (this to his younger brother) "you are full of crap!"

"Mom, this cake is crap-a-licious!" You can imagine how tired I was of that word after just one day. Then, at thirteen, fourteen and fifteen he was allowed another word each birthday. At fifteen, it was "hell." I figure people even say that one in some churches. The ministers, especially. I won't say what words my son is now allowed, at sixteen, to use. He uses good judgment about where and when to use the words, after the actual day of his birthday. No, he is still not allowed to say the mother of all cuss words. Eighteen. I knew that was your next question.

I'm trying to cut way back on my cussing, especially since now I'm working in a church, and it takes people aback when their minister doesn't speak pleasantly. They are a loving and forgiving group, but I don't want to put that to the test very often. Sometimes, though, it satisfies the soul and makes the heart light to just cut loose. In the car, all alone, with the windows rolled up. Because, you all know, the car is where you're allowed to say all those words. However, if the thought of a minister cussing is offensive to you, and if you see me on the road with my mouth moving, I'm singing along with the radio. That's my story and I'm sticking to it.

TEMPLE OF THE DMV
❖

 Early in the morning, Spartanburg, SC. We were a
mother and a son waiting together. This was an
important day. The feeling was of sitting in the
temple of a solemn religion. Young men and women
of the region come to this temple with their hearts,
their futures, their well being held in trembling
hands. They are here for a rite of passage. The tests
are difficult. The stakes are high. We are at the
Department of Motor Vehicles, waiting to take the
driver's license test. The atmosphere is hushed,
heavy with portent. If you are deemed worthy, you
may cross the threshold into adulthood. You will
have freedom, motion, independence. The
priestesses move slowly but with purpose behind a
waist high wall. A disembodied voice coos
overhead: "Now serving number 315 at window 12.
Number 315 at window 12."

Obstacles have been set and overcome. We have
had the proper preparatory classes. Tests of
eyesight and memory have been completed. We
have the right pieces of paper. As in the old stories
where the young ones are told to gather one
feather from the phoenix that flies out of the east

on winter solstice, one berry from the bush that sits high on the west side of yonder mountain, one vial of water from the dew on the first rose of summer. We have the correct insurance information. We have the right dates on our applications. We have had the permit for the required length of time. All is in order.

Parents sit nearby their young men and women, trying to be encouraging without being intrusive. Allowing the young people to retain their essential coolness, which is, after all what they believe will take them through the test. Did they study the book? In this religion, study of the book is essential. They don't always do it, though, believing that their coolness will carry them farther than it actually will. Did they practice? Some got behind the wheel and pulled into the space between the two sawhorses at the high school, parallel parking until they were masterful. Some did not. Some studied the book but did not practice driving. Some have driven in the fields since they were thirteen but have not opened the book.

Then the time is at hand. The tester comes to gather your young person, to take them to the threshold, to put him or her through the test of knowledge, skill and endurance. Some testers seem to want the young person to do well. Some smile when the young person forgets to pull up the emergency brake when parking as if for the whole night. The tester smiles when the young person pulls around a bicyclist as she has seen her father do time and time again. This young person fails the test.

If the young people fail, will they lower their head and acknowledge that they should have practiced, that they should have studied the book? Probably not. They will blame the tester. They may utter angry words and make fearsome gestures. They may cry. Maybe this shows they don't yet have the maturity to cross the threshold. Maybe this is how the parent behaves as well. Maybe the parent resolves to work harder on character formation, on correct behavior. Maybe it is too late. They wrestle together with the issues raised by the trials they have passed through. The threshold will be approached again.

If the young people pass the test, there is feasting and celebration, solemn speeches about responsibility and heartfelt congratulations. Another one is launched. The opponents have been worthy, as has been your young one. Adulthood is

BRAHMA BULL, KNIVES, FLU SHOTS, FAMILY

❖

It was my cousin Lila's year to be host for the annual reunion my mother's family holds every Thanksgiving, so about sixty of us were gathering at her house. She had written to ask if I would bring sweet potato casserole and say the prayer before dinner. That was brave of her. Not the casserole part—I make a mean sweet potato casserole. It was brave of her to ask me to be the one to pray. Many older members of that side of the family are pillars of an ethnic Scottish Presbyterian denomination that doesn't yet allow women to be ministers. Lila and her mother have been working for years to try to change that, but you know how churches hate to change. Most relatives of my mother's generation approach the fact of my being a minister in the way of the Southern culture, which is to say they ignore it, as they would if I wore an outlandish outfit, a really bad haircut or had an unfortunate lapse in manners.

Coming into the enormous front room around noon with my sons, Kiya and our sweet potato casserole, we saw knives gleaming on every bookcase and coffee table. Uncle Norman, 82, had recently returned from Pakistan, from the area where he and my mother had grown up as missionary kids. He'd brought back a collection of Gurkha weapons. There were kukris of every length, dangerous curved blades whispering of battles long past. Lila's twelve-year-old son Decker was running out through the carved Mexican door to the screen porch brandishing a long talwar sword, chasing his squealing sister Emma into the back yard. No one seemed overly concerned. Since half the adults there were doctors and the other half were lawyers, I figured that if anything happened we could sort it out, so I set the casserole down on the side board and drifted over to where Norman was holding forth on his trip, on the bravery of the Gurkhas, and on the beauty of the Himalayas.

Glancing out into the yard to keep an eye on the chase, I was dumbstruck. An enormous Brahma bull was being led around out there by a woman dressed like a rodeo cowgirl. Her blue vest sparkled with silver stars. The 2,000-pound animal was speckled gray and white, with a hump on his shoulders and a dewlap hanging from his neck, flapping from side to side as he plodded behind her wearing the expression of an ancient being praying for world peace. I was glad somebody was praying for peace. My guess is that when the bull saw

Decker and Emma run out of the house, his prayer for peace got a lot more specific.

This particular bull's job in the world, apparently, was to give slow rides to people. Helping people face their fears is a good way to work for peace, I think. Most of us rode the bull that day, except the most elderly generation. They watched and applauded in the cool sunshine. Even cousin Tigger was coaxed tenderly out of her wheelchair and onto his broad back.

Uncle Henry used to pray before dinner every year, a long and sonorous prayer that reminded God about the Puritans and the Native Americans (whose genes, I suspect, dance within the DNA of this family), a prayer that named one by one the blessings of this land and this family. My prayer, the first ever given at this gathering by a woman minister, was of gratitude for the land, for the family, for the love that surrounded us. I invited those present to call the names of those we missed, those who weren't able to be there or who had died. One or two cousins said "good job," Lila and her mother did, of course. Most of them smiled past me as if I hadn't spoken.

The food and the company were a pleasure. We told stories of long-ago mischief and mischief accomplished since last Thanksgiving. One of my favorite cousins and his wife told me about entertaining the devout and extremely dull president of a southern Christian college, along with his extremely dull wife. They had invited a couple of our livelier cousins to the dinner to make it more bearable, and one of those, stunned into an episode of bad judgment by being bored to slobber, had attempted to improve the evening by slipping Amaretto liqueur into his and his wife's after-dinner coffee.

Through an unfortunate mix-up, the devout president's wife was served doctored coffee, and throughout the rest of the evening she pestered my cousin's wife to tell her where she got this coffee. "This is s-o-o-o delicious," she cooed dreamily, "what kind of coffee is this?" The two who were in the know shook the sofa with suppressed giggles, almost falling against one another.

My cousin's wife said "I couldn't let her see them laughing, so I finally turned to the woman and held. Her. Gaze." Her open hands went to the sides of her face, like a horse's blinders. "I held her gaze so she wouldn't see them falling into one another over there, and I told her, 'I grind my own beans!'"

After dinner we all lined up, as always, for flu shots. This strikes strangers as odd, but we are used to it. One of the doctor cousins brings a cooler full of medicine and doses everyone in a back bedroom with the help of his ten-year-old daughter. She's a whiz with the alcohol and cotton swabs. It's community building, getting a chance to be brave together after dinner.

Thanksgiving, for me, is the family. I have taken my sons to this gathering every year since they were born. Now I take my beautiful partner, and many of the family members are supportive. I am grateful for the tradition, the talent, the wildness, the faith, character, and kindness of these people. They have their faults, their self-righteousness, and their blind spots. Don't we all? It is a blessing to carry them in my heart. I wish adventures, peace, good company, and good mischief for us all.

SING ME TO SLEEP

❖

In college, Emmie from Texas was one of my best friends. We roomed together in a rickety white house with a big porch. Three of us slept in the back bedroom and two other young women took the one in the front. Emmie had a wide smile and long brown hair, and she could sing high and sweet like the princesses in Disney cartoons. I teased her, saying I always expected little bluebirds to come flutter around her head. Emmie's eyebrows would jump when she hit the highest notes. Even the way she talked was singing. She seemed effortlessly slender, for which I would normally have hated her, but you couldn't hate Emmie. She was a sweet and smart deeply religious person who could also tell a good dirty joke. She loved sitting cross-legged on the floor, and sometimes she laughed so hard she would fall backwards and kick her feet in the air.

When I got the phone call about my mother having been diagnosed with breast cancer, Mama was 45. My grandmother, on the phone, said the cancer was in an advanced stage, but the doctors were going to try chemo and radiation. After I hung up, the news left a roaring in my ears. For days, I couldn't hear anything right. The only thing that soothed me was to be in the middle of a group of friends talking to one another without expecting me to participate, letting the sounds of their conversation wash over and around me. Emmie was one of the ones who took care of me in those weeks after the phone call.

One night I was sad and agitated, mad at God for letting cancer happen to my mom, mad at a deeper, unacknowledged level at my mother for detecting a lump and waiting a year to go to the doctor. I didn't have the two things available to me that usually made things better: talking to God and talking to my mother. Emmie and I had been playing our guitars and singing. After a while I lay on my bed and asked if she would sing to me until I fell asleep.

Usually when someone sings to me I want to tell them how beautiful it sounds; I want to thank them for doing it; I want them to know that I appreciate them and that I'm listening all the way through. That night, in pain, I needed not to do any of those normal things. I needed to be able to accept that gift from her in silence and go to sleep.

I remember lying in bed in such misery I wanted to crawl out of my skin, out of my body and away. My mother was going through something really bad far, far away from me. She told me to stay at school, that she would be fine. Guiltily, I knew I wanted to stay at school. I must be a terrible person. I wanted to go be with my mom, and I wanted not to be there. I wanted things to go back to normal. I wanted none of this to be happening.

Whenever my eyelids would flutter open as I was drowsing, I saw Emmie sitting across the room on her bed, bent over her guitar, her eyes closed, singing to me. My mother wasn't fine. She wasn't going to be fine, and the singing was the only thing that night that held any comfort.

She sang to me past the time when I fell asleep. I don't know when she stopped singing. I have been grateful to her since then for that gift, and I think of it often. She is an Episcopal priest now, one of the downtown New York clergy who worked for weeks on end after 9/11. I imagine them with their hearts torn into ragged pieces, their hands and voices still giving comfort. Maybe once in a while, they sang to the survivors.

These days, as part of my spiritual strengthening, I'm trying the Buddhist practice of being open to the sufferings of others without trying to take it on or fix them or make it all stop. Suffering is hard to take in. I want to look away.

I see my therapy client whose parents snatched all the beauty from his life day after day from the moment of his birth; I see the mahogany-skinned teenage boys on the front steps of the house that looks uninhabitable; I see the widow at my church whose daughter has come to pack her up and take her home with her, far from anyone else she knows, far from the life that was hers. I practice looking. I don't know how to fix any of it.

After years of mothering, of being a therapist, of watching the news, and ministering in churches, my heart is torn and ragged, too. Pain and love tumble over one another. Both surround me. People sing to me in so many ways through the tumult of this life. My sons sing to me, with their voices and with their lives. My sweetheart sings to me true and strong. My friends sing to me from nearby and far away. The people I've worked among sing to me. I know you have sung to people in your time. The world itself is singing. I'm singing, too. Close your eyes for a while. We're right here.

WISDOM TREE

I dragged myself to an early morning theme talk even though it was the last day of a week at church camp and I was tired from staying up late singing with friends and dancing my fool head off. A panel of old-timers was gathered. They were taking about the early days of this camp that now had grown to about a thousand Unitarian Universalists coming together every July on the campus of Virginia Tech. Here is the story that stuck in my mind. There was a teacher who used to come to the camp every summer, a man who could become Thomas Jefferson, Ralph Waldo Emerson, or Theodore Parker. He would bring his class to sit under a large oak tree out on the quad, and the conversation would range over history, philosophy and theology. Summer after summer folks would look forward to that class, to sitting under what they came to call "the wisdom tree," they would look forward to having the kind of conversations where you hear and say things that surprise and delight you. One summer night, during the church camp, a storm came through. As the people slept, winds and rain whipped the campus. Lightning flashed and struck hard. It struck close. In the morning, daylight revealed the wisdom tree scattered in splinters on the ground. As the grounds crew came to clear it away, church people came from every corner of the campus to circle round. One by one they asked to take a piece of the tree home with them.

This story struck me deep. I think that there is wisdom available to us, and that it shows up in history, in theology, poetry, music, art, scripture, conversation, nature and ritual. Individuals have a spark of the Divine inside, an inner wisdom that, related to sanely, responsibly, and in community, will lead each person to truth and peace.

Sometimes the place you used to find wisdom gets destroyed. People fail you, a church disappoints you, new information strips away your feeling about a scripture. It's as if your wisdom tree is lying in splinters. We are tempted to take our piece of wisdom home with us and put it in a place of honor, savoring and celebrating the little piece of wisdom we have, pulling it out whenever there is a new question, a new issue, acting as if that piece of wisdom is self-sustaining, and as if it is enough, on its own, to sustain us. Acting like this, we are forgetting the crucial next step. What is needed is to bring our piece of the wisdom tree back together with the others and stand together on the roots of our wisdom tree, on the roots of what wisdom we have. We do have it inside us, but it is not enough to hold and savor just the one piece. It needs to be added to the others. You can't walk a good spiritual path all by yourself. You have to be in relationship to a community. Your wisdom needs to have fresh life breathed into it by touching it, again and again to its Source, by bringing it together with the piece of wisdom others carry with them. Then if lightning strikes, if all the places you used to go are ruined, just hold up your piece and we'll find each other.

UNICORN

I saw a unicorn coming at me on I-85. That's what it looked like at first glance, anyway. Don't get me wrong, I'm a sensible person. I know there aren't such things in the world, but there it was, this enormous gray ridged horn coming fast toward me southbound, and it was angled forward and up, as if pointing to the Blue Ridge Mountains and, after that, the sky. As it blew by me I saw that it was a church steeple on a flatbed truck, being shipped to its new church building.

The odd sight stuck with me. I started thinking about the church group that was getting that steeple. I wondered how much it cost, and I thought about all the things it symbolized. Most basically, the steeple symbolizes the church pointing to God. We all know that God is not literally "up there;" a lot of us think of God as everywhere, and that's just the beginning of all of our various thoughts on the nature of the One.

I asked myself what would be a better symbol of pointing to God. What direction(s) would it point? It might look like one of those Moravian stars with almost as many points as a chrysanthemum.

I wonder why people wanted to build one more church when there are already so many. Sometimes the reason is a growing population of people who need you, and no church of your kind is near them, so you build one. Sometimes the reason is a split in an existing church, and one unhappy, hurt, and angry group is making a new church where they can become the community they want to be. "All it takes," someone once told me, "is a grievance and a coffee pot."

I thought about how much hope it takes to build a church. "This time," they might be thinking, "this time we will get it right. We will be good people and we will really point folks toward God and there won't be politics or infighting or cliques and we won't ever disappoint each other, and we won't do things in a slap-dash manner, and this, finally, will be the church we have all been dreaming about. We won't fight about silly things like carpet or moving the piano or the banners. We'll be kind and respectful of one another, challenging one another lovingly, cleaning up our own hearts before we start trying to clean up other people's hearts, and it will be like it's supposed to be."

I thought about how, from my perspective, a church like the one they may be hoping for is as mythic and elusive a creature as the unicorn. Churches cause lots of joy, but they also cause pain as they strive to improve people, as they strive to instruct people on the right and wrong ways of being a person in this world. Some say: "Don't ever drink, but you may wear jewelry and makeup." Some say: "Absolutely no vanity or fancy dress, but you may drink beer, as it's one of God's gifts."

Some churches talk lots about hell and others don't mention it, even though it's there, undergirding everything. People try to be kind but often, when we feel passionately about something, it is hard to keep in mind that the other people are more important than correctness of behavior or purity of doctrine. A conviction that the loving God they worship will punish mistakes with eternal hellfire can make some people feel an urgency that comes across as meanness.

Some churches are kind but ineffectual, and some are kind and powerful and they do lots of good and they function in marvelous ways.

Churches are like families. Present are the relatives who drive you nuts, the misunderstandings that hurt, and all the destructive behavior that families can have. At church you also get the warmth, growth, shared history, support and love you can find in a family. People act like people no matter where we are. We know we are supposed to be kind and loving and not jump down each other's throats for not getting the right kind of free-trade coffee. We know we're not supposed to fight bitterly about the best ways to work for peace. I heard a poem on the radio the other day, part of which was a prayer: "God make the bad people good and the good people nice."

Honey, we're trying.

WISH YOU WERE HERE
❖

 The church was having its monthly music jam, and the regulars were there. Doug plays fiddle, and his teenage son Owen brought his electric guitar. Owen was in his Marilyn Manson t-shirt. It's usually that or a shirt with vintage picture of David Bowie. Ed, who is my age, late forties, plays mandolin. Other folks brought guitars and drums. Some came to sing harmony. We went around the circle, taking turns starting a song; then the others would join in. Most of the folks my age were playing folk music. Since it was at my church, cheesy songs about froggies were outlawed, and it was a Kumbaya-free-zone. I tried to ban John Denver, but you have to pick your battles. We had played John Hiatt, Emmylou Harris, some Rolling Stones, Indigo Girls, Appalachian sex and death songs, and a couple of old gospel things.

We had just finished "Angel Band," and it was Owen's turn. Head down, be fingered the strings while we waited to see what he would play. I don't know if he was feeling shy, or if his energy had been sapped by an overdose of folk music. His dad said "Come on, Owen, play that Pink Floyd thing you were working on. Owen's fingers found the opening riff to "Wish You Were Here." Then he sighed, and all the wind seemed to go out of his sails. He muttered, "No, I'll pass, I guess."

"Don't do that," Ed said, and started to pick out the notes on his mandolin. Owen's dad picked up the notes on the fiddle. Owen's head came up and he started the chords. We tried to figure out when to jump in "So, so you think you can tell ..." We had come in at the wrong place. Owen gave an exaggerated nod to show us the beat. He said, "NOW," and we began again.

"Heaven from hell? Blue skies from pain..." By the end of the song we were all grinning like fools. Yeah. Pink Floyd on the fiddle, mandolin and electric guitar, a sixteen year old and a forty six year old playing a song about a feeling everyone has sometimes. That's what I'm talking about. We had church. Wish you'd been there.

IN THE BATHTUB, BETWEEN THE SHEETS

I have gone to a lot of church services in my time. Wearing Mary Jane shoes and white stockings when I was eight, in a blue coat with a velveteen collar my mother had made, sitting next to my little sister in her coat, identical to mine, trying not to wiggle in the pew, making check marks as the sections of the order of service finished: hymn number one, pastoral prayer, scripture reading, sermon. I loved checking off the sermon. My cousin Ed occasionally slipped a transistor radio in his pocket and ran the earphones up through his shirt so you could barely see the wire carrying music or a ball game to his ear. Big plain windows, eggshell walls, red carpet. I think the most exciting thing that ever happened in church was when the man in front of me held so still that during the entire service a small spider was able to spin a web in the angle of his neck, stretching the silk from his ear to the shoulder of his gray suit, making a perfect design that was only disturbed when he shuffled to his feet to sing the last hymn.

We colored in our bulletins and we looked through the hymnals and made ourselves giggle by adding "between the sheets" to their titles. A Baptist friend says she and her friends added "in the bathtub." "Turn Back, O Man" between the sheets. "We Three Kings of Orient Are" in the bathtub.

Years ago I came into Unitarian Universalism, a community of a freer faith. I'm home. I listen to people talk sometimes about liberal religion, that it's a thin gruel, watered down to please everyone. Our seven Principles, they complain, are either too much like a creed or so general as to be meaningless.

My experience of the Principles is that they are deeply demanding. The first one asks me to affirm and promote the inherent worth and dignity of every person, which means that I can no longer subscribe to the cheerful Calvinist doctrine of the total depravity of human nature. At first hearing the doctrine sounds grim, but really, if you are in fact starting with a totally depraved nature, opportunities for self-congratulation abound: "Hey, I didn't knock over a 7-eleven this afternoon, even though money's pretty tight. I'm doing well!" Now I have to struggle with the worth and dignity of people who do unspeakably awful things, whereas the doctrine of total depravity made that one a no-brainer. I'm supposed to value the democratic process, hearing the voice of everyone equally, allowing everyone to have a say.

The UU Principles are demanding enough to make me whine. For those who feel they are thin gruel, I have a suggestion. Let's stick something onto the end of every principle that will stop people from smiling and nodding comfortably as they are read. Instead of adding "in the bathtub," or "between the sheets," how about attaching: "beginning in our homes and congregations?" Then we'd be faced with affirming things like "the goal of ...peace, liberty and justice for all, beginning in our homes and congregations." Everyone who has raised children knows that peace is often at odds with liberty, and that justice demands a disturbance of the peace. To put those three together in one principle is outrageously hopeful. To paint a picture of a whole world of peace and justice is easier than to think about it in a context of Cheerios and pajamas, car keys and cleaning up one's bedroom.

"Justice, equity and compassion in human relations, beginning in our homes and congregations" is a sobering ideal. I don't know about you, but I have sat in meetings about right relations and seen well-meaning people get testy with one another. Some of the nastiest behavior I've seen was at a community workshop for peace activists.

Lao Tzu, quoted in the back of our hymnbook, tells me that peace in the world begins with peace in the home, which begins with peace in the heart. If I start with my own heart, the demands of our principles get even heavier. Peace and compassion in my heart? Justice too? Freedom as well? Affirming the worth of every person all the time, not only with my words and my behavior but in my secret heart? If we added "in the heart" to the Principles, they might as well just read "Be Jesus" and be done with it. I'm sorry I even brought that heart thing up.

For me, the pulse point of the faith is being connected to something greater than myself, wallowing in the Spirit of Life, Love and Truth, having Fair Trade coffee and important conversations, standing for love, standing against quibbling, complaining, flouncing off and being easily offended, moving toward being in right relationship with ourselves, one another, and the planet. For me, this faith is not a thin gruel. It's not even a rich and hearty gruel. It's walnuts and bananas, pancakes, mangoes, arugula, ginger and avocado. The feast is prepared with effort, enjoyment, persistence and commitment. Care to join me?

THE BOARD OR THE *ILLUMINATI*
❖

 My father was a news analyst and commentator for our local CBS station, on the six and eleven o'clock news every night. When he first started the job, he said, he used to stand by the Associated Press news ticker and weep over the stories of cruelty and disaster typed in black ink on the white paper tape spooling through his fingers onto the floor.

Once in a while he would wonder aloud to me about whether there might be a group of people orchestrating world events. Intelligent people he knew, he said, believed that a secret group called the Illuminati was behind the wars and rumors of wars, the coups and the oil prices, terrorist attacks, uprisings and assassinations. He was almost willing to believe that there might be a secret cabal or two attempting to control events. Why would there be only one? Wasn't it more in the nature of things for there to be at least two? Even the town you live in has more than one group trying to control things. I know that it is comforting for some to believe that men and women who are hugely intelligent and capable are in control, whether or not they are good people. If the Illuminati are in charge of world events, you may as well sit back in your recliner and watch large men rebuild motorcycles on television because it's out of your hands, anyway.

I thought about the Illuminati the other day when I was talking to a friend who is a parish minister. He told the story of standing between pews after the Sunday service. A few people were still in the room, milling around. He was having a conversation with a couple of members about a piece of donated art. It was a painting of questionable quality. There was a large tree, an owl and a window, and the owl looked like it was suffering from a stomachache and was beyond the point at which it could bear up and maintain its good character. Should they display the painting? Everyone loved the donor, who had painted it with love in her heart, but opinions were mixed about where it could go.

"We should let the Décor Committee decide," one of them said.

The next Sunday after services, the minister was buttonholed by two members who looked upset and angry.

"We have been talking about this all week, and we thought it was time to get the whole thing out on the table. You need to come clean with us right now about it, because the way this church is doing things is not right! You can't have things run by some secret Core Committee that only some people know about, and that no regular members know how to get on, and it's not even democratic, to have this secret committee that makes all the decisions while the rest of us just twiddle our thumbs and read the board minutes like that's going to give us a real picture of what's going on!"

Stunned and mystified by this request, the minister struggled to find a way to participate in this conversation.

"What? What makes you think there is a secret committee that runs things?"

"We heard you talking about it last Sunday after the service. You stood right there with Myrtle and Henry and told them the decision needed to go to the Core Committee, and when I heard that, I knew that what I'd always suspected was true: that there was a group of people who run this place and that everything else is just for show."

The minister thought to himself, "Core committee . . core committee, Myrtle and Henry . . . What were we talking about after church last Sunday? Oh! The donated art that nobody likes! And what did we say about it? That the decision should be made by the Décor Committee . . ."

"Décor Committee!" he cried out. "We were talking about that lovely piece that was donated and what to do with it, and we said the decision should be made by the Décor Committee."

I remember the shock of realizing for the first time that the President of the United States and I were the same age. That is a job that one just naturally hopes will be filled by a completely grown adult with wisdom and experience. Often it was an adult with whom I disagreed, and adult I felt was doing a terrible job, an adult I suspected was a bad person, but it was an at least someone whose brain was more developed than mine, whose sense of the world was larger, whose life experience prepared him for the shocks of day to day word events. On the day I realized he and I were the same age I was catapulted into a world where no one wiser than I was in charge. At best, the ones running things were just ordinary humans struggling to think what to do, much in the same way that my friends and I would try to think what to do. Most of my friends would say they didn't feel completely grown up. Who was grown up, then, if not the President of the United States? Would he secretly say to his friends that he didn't feel completely grown up? On that day I had to grow up completely or else live in a world with no grownups at all.

It's a scary place when you know that, at best, ordinary women and men like you are making the biggest decisions there are. How much more comforting to live in a world where gray haired Illuminati who have the wisdom of ages handed down to them by the Illuminati before them are pulling the strings of the world's economies, governments, directing the flow of arms and uranium, fanning and then dampening the fires of conflict among the world's religions, controlling trade, food, water, and air. Maybe they are benevolent and maybe they just want to get rich, but at least they know what they are doing.

Is all of this related to the desire to believe that God is in control everything? As playwright Archibald MacLeish famously wrote in his play about Job, J.B., "If God is God, he is not good. If God is good, he is not God." A person can just look at the world the way it is and be struck with that. I know there are people, though, who would rather believe in a God who is all-powerful and in control than a God who wouldn't want horrors to happen but cannot prevent them. Other people would rather not believe in God at all in order to avoid the whole dilemma. I don't think there is anyone in control of the whole shebang. I don't even think there is anyone in charge, which is quite different but still alarming. I do believe in a larger mystery, a power greater than myself, and it might be called love, or it might be called truth, or I might call it God but whatever it is, we are its hands and feet and its voice. Better get cracking and step up, start helping that President, helping the Board at church, better start weighing in as decisions are made about trade and food and water. We can still let the Décor Committee decide where to hang the painting of the tree, the window and the dyspeptic owl.

EASTER AT HONEY SPRINGS UU

❖

The Worship Planning Group at Honey Springs Unitarian Universalist Congregation—a mythical UU congregation where we are all the way we are, only more so—was seated around the table in Classroom #6 discussing the upcoming Easter Intergenerational service. Someone had put a scented candle in the chalice, and the room was beginning to list a little to the raspberry side. The Rev. Cotton Lovingood, the new minister, was having a little trouble breathing, and briefly wondered if it would be seen as sacrilegious to ask if they could put the chalice out for the rest of the meeting. Mindful of his previous two very brief settlements since seminary, and wanting to have a brightly successful ministry here at Honey Springs, he decided to endure.

"It's in the name," a tall woman dressed in gauzy green layers was saying. "Easter is from Eostre or Ostara, the Saxon goddess of spring. In ancient Greece she was called Astarte, in Assyria she was called Ishtar. Hear it? Easter, Ishtar, it's the same word. Her worshippers would have egg hunts at dawn on the day of the Equinox, and the rabbits were sacred to her, too." She looked at the minister.

"Easter is about Jesus, people!" A slender young man leaned both of his forearms on the table. "Why is it so hard just to let the church talk about Jesus once in a while? Is Honey Springs going to be like that place where the only time the name of Jesus is uttered is when the minister stubs his toe?" He looked at the minister.

"Let's just have a Flower Communion and be done with it," a blue-eyed man in his seventies said, spreading his open hands and smiling. "Norbert Capek invented it as a purely Unitarian ritual, so I say we use it and teach the children to be Unitarians." He looked at the minister.

"Unitarian Universalists," a couple of people murmured, with the air of barely realizing they had spoken aloud.

Wondering if it was time for him to say something, Cotton Lovingood scrunched his toes against the cork bed of his Birkenstocks. He opened his mouth, but an elderly woman in the corner beat him to it. Her name was Phoebe Something-or-Other.

Impeccable British accent. (Cotton's mother would have fallen upon her like a long-lost sister.

(Cotton's mother had been a shameless Anglophile.) "The Langari people didn't have spring, but every time the river flooded they made a nice stew of rabbit with a puree of mashed fire ants for a bit of zing. When Adrian and I were living with them we used to watch them try to keep the little ants in the mortars long enough to get mashed. Used to take bets in the beginning, Adrian did, on the ratio of dead ants to stings. Of course the cooks were highly skilled." Everyone looked at her. Cotton couldn't remember what he'd been about to say.

"Easter is about resurrection," he began.

"Yes, new life! Green shoots! Bulbs!"

"The resurrection of Jesus. A particular resurrection," said the young man.

"You don't really believe in that literally, do you?" the blue-eyed man asked.

Cotton held up his hand. "Tell me what the resurrection of Jesus means to you," he asked the young man.

"Well, he was dead and now he's alive—in our hearts. The Christ-principle is an engine of love and compassion in the world, and love can't be destroyed. That's what it means to me."

"So, love lives on?" Cotton asked.

"How can that be true?" sighed the woman in green. "Love ends. Everyone's been in a relationship where love ended."

"But love itself," the young man stretched his hands toward her imploringly. "Love itself can't be destroyed. It emerges like a green weed from the tiniest crack in the cement, and if there is no crack it will make one."

"We could give the children seeds, I suppose," the woman said. "Life, like love itself, unable to be destroyed.

"We're destroying life as we sit here," the man at the end of the table said. "Do you know what the carbon footprint of this building is?"

"Love itself," Cotton repeated.

"Yes," the young man said. "And that is a perfect theme for an intergenerational Easter service. You all have got to stop marginalizing the Christians."

"Isn't that what the Flower Communion is about, too?" the man at the end of the table said. "We are all different. We don't have to think alike to love alike? The strength of nature to stand up to the way it's been treated these past two hundred years. And—speaking of marginalized! The Humanists are being pushed out of this movement by Christians and astrologers."

Cotton smiled. "I would certainly say love is at the center for me."

"So you're a Humanist like I am," the man said. "I'm a Humanist UU, and Jill is a Pagan UU. Jim is a Christian UU, and Phoebe is an anthropologist."

"Oh, I don't know if I'm just pagan," said the woman in green. "I like Jesus just fine. I have felt marginalized about that. Well, about being Pagan, too," she said, with the look of wounded righteousness that can bring a whole roomful of UUs to their knees.

"I certainly could do without hearing about Jesus any more for the rest of my life," said the anthropologist emphatically. "So what are you?"

Cotton sighed. "Listen," he said, "I'm just a plain old middle-of-the-road Unitarian Universalist. I think the human spirit is magnificent, and science is a great way to think about the world. It has limitations, though, and I'm comfortable with the idea of mystery, even mystery that may never be understood. The teachings of Rabbi Jesus are fine with me, especially the Sermon on the Mount, which, if it were all the scripture a person had, would be plenty to go on for an entire life. I feel connected with nature, and I think humans live more richly when they learn how the earth works, when they dance by bonfires at night, when they have a sense of awe at the wonders that inhabit this planet and beyond. I do not think that nature is sweet, nice, benevolent, or motherly, though. You'd have to have stayed indoors your whole life to believe that."

His voice was beginning to rise.

"I also like to practice paying attention to my breathing and detaching from outcomes, but that doesn't make me a Buddhist. I'm UU, which means I have access to all of that, and the freedom to draw on all of it. Unitarian Universalism is more than our history. It's a big tent with room enough for me to have the faith I've just laid out and for you to have the faiths you've laid out, too, and we can all just call ourselves Unitarian Universalists and imagine ourselves at the center of this big free faith and not squeezed into its corners feeling marginalized." His fingers had made sarcastic air-quotes around the word. He hated air-quotes, and here he was doing it. Wasn't that always the way? The anthropologist looked at him for the first time. The others suddenly became fascinated by the top of the table.

"So you want to do something about love's power to create new life?" he continued meekly. That would be wonderful, everyone agreed.

The members of the planning group managed to get over their surprise at the new minister's outburst, and they planned a nice mash-up of Passover, Easter, flowers, love, diversity, and new life. One of the readings and one of the hymns mentioned Jesus or the tomb. After the meeting the young man and the woman in green got to talking about relationships that had gone wrong. The blue-eyed man gave the anthropologist a ride back to her apartment. Cotton went home and wrote PATIENCE on a sticky note and put it on the bathroom mirror. Then he thought about the kindness of the people, about their being at an evening meeting they hadn't been paid to come to, about their quickness to forgive his somewhat edgy description of his own faith, and he realized that wasn't the whole truth about the meeting. He took another sticky note and wrote GRATITUDE.

HONEY SPRINGS' ANT PROBLEM

❖

One Sunday morning after the service at Honey Springs Unitarian Universalist Congregation—a mythical UU congregation where we are all the way we are, only more so—a small knot of people was sending out waves of emotional turbulence in the hallway. One dad held his three-year-old daughter in his arms as her mom patted her back, calming her shuddering breaths. Another mom held her seven-year-old by the hand. He wanted to go, and he didn't want to be seen holding his mother's hand, so every now and then he would try to tug free.

"Well, we can't have the kids covered in ants when they're on the playground, Craig," said Gail, the Honey Springs director of Lifespan Religious Education. Stooping over so he could hear her well, Craig, the tall, retired pilot who headed up the Building and Grounds Committee, nodded energetically. The mother and father nodded, too. "Aren't they just around the edges of the playground, though?" Craig asked. "Just in the ivy that covers the fence? We don't want to spray poison on the playground and get the kids get covered in neurotoxins, now, do we?" No one wanted that. You could tell there wasn't one person in the hall that was in favor of covering the kids in neurotoxins.

"You are going to have to Do Something," Gail said. You could hear the capital letters as she spoke. She didn't quite stamp her foot, but almost. "You could just spray along the fence line and I'll keep the kids away from the ivy. How's that?"

"I don't know, Gail. I think you're attacking a gnat with a howitzer here."

The boy's mom spoke up. "They were here first, guys. We built on top of them, and they have a right to be here just as much as we do. The kids can get used to just brushing them off. Coexisting with nature is a really good lesson for them. They don't have to annihilate everything that makes them uncomfortable."

Gail opened her mouth to reply, then shut it again. The Rev. Cotton Lovingood, the new minister, was standing in the door to his office, watching their exchange. Gail didn't know what his position on ant-killing would be. Perhaps he was one of those who shooed spiders out of his house, blew mosquitoes off of his arm with a gentle breath of air, trapped mice and drove them to the nearest state park to let them go scampering into the underbrush to take their chances in the wild. He was married, but Gail didn't know his wife Laura that well, and they had no kids. For all she knew Cotton and Laura didn't mind at all being covered in ants. She pictured them on a hiking trail, eating sandwiches, packing out the bio-degradable brown paper in which the sandwiches had been wrapped, laughing gently as they brushed tiny congregations of picnic ants off one another's arms and legs.

Mostly Craig liked to handle everything by himself. He detested meetings, and he didn't like calling around asking people to help. Sometimes they said "no," and sometimes they said "yes" but didn't show up, and it was just disheartening. Plus, they wanted to talk everything to death, and he would just rather get it done. Sometimes, when he didn't want to be part of what was happening around him, Craig's mind would go back up into the sky, 30,000 feet above the noise and tussle of ground level, and he would barely see the people clamoring for attention, for a solution. Gail was a fine person, she was just easily stirred up, Craig thought, and she seemed to feel that all she had to say was, "It's for the children," and everyone should drop whatever they were doing and fix what she wanted fixed.

Craig was a fine person, Gail thought, but he was hard to pin down. That man could think for three months about something and apparently not notice the passage of time. These ants were a persistent problem, and every spring they made trouble. Two years ago they got into the motion sensors in the Parish House alarm system, and the police kept getting called in the middle of the night. Little boogers. The ants, not the police. Two years ago the peace lily in the minister's office sprouted a tiny line of ants traveling from its terra cotta pot, up the wall, and out into the back garden. When the minister picked up the pot to see where they were coming from, thousands of ants erupted from the pot where they had overwintered, covering her hands and arms. To her credit, she didn't drop the pot until she got out the front door, and then ants, dirt, and terra cotta went everywhere. Gail wasn't too sure that wasn't why that minister had left for another congregation.

In staff meeting that Tuesday, Cotton, Gail, and Shameeka, the administrator, were talking about the ant problem. Shameeka had been at the church for many years, through three ministers. Cotton had been caught up on the ant history, the motion detectors, the police, and the mouse in the kitchen. One minister had been so tenderhearted that he had insisted that the mouse in the kitchen remain unmolested. He even learned to enjoy its bright little eyes as it watched him make tea in the afternoon. That minister had waxed eloquent, Shameeka reported, about non-harming as a tenet of spiritual practice and said he was working on a sermon about his conversations with the mouse about Jesus and the Buddha. She had simply kept her office door closed during the mouse's tenure.

One autumn afternoon a stout black snake had come into the building, lured by the mouse's scent. Preparations for a reception were underway that afternoon as a memorial service was taking place; the Women's Alliance was in charge of the refreshment table. Buckie McClaren had opened a low cabinet door to find a few platters and came across the fat snake resting after enjoying the mouse for its dinner. Fortunately the bagpiper chose that exact moment to expel a loud burst of sound from the pipes in preparation for his moving rendition of "Amazing Grace," so no one in the service heard Buckie cuss. She had been in the Army and had quite a salty tongue.

Cotton enquired about what had happened to the snake.

"Oh, Buckie took care of it. Grabbed that thing behind its head and marched it outside. Tossed it over the fence into the neighbor's back yard. They moved away a couple of years later. It had nothing to do with the snake," Shameeka said. The three of them nodded silently, the way you do when you have no idea what to say next.

"What should we do about the ants?" Gail asked Cotton.

"What are our options?" he asked them both.

"I wouldn't want my grandbabies covered in ants, but neither would I want them covered in poison," Shameeka said, shaking her head.

"I say we just treat the playground on a Monday so the ants have time to die and the poison dissipates before the kids get back onto the playground the next Sunday. Craig does not have to know."

"We could just poke the ant bait into holes in the ground real close to the fence rather than scatter it on the playground," Shameeka thought out loud.

"You probably think we should just let them be, don't you?" Gail asked Cotton wearily.

"You don't think maybe they're just living there under the fence, praying for world peace?" Cotton asked.

"But they sting," Gail said.

"Bite, I think it is, " Shameeka said, "but still ."

"Hard to believe they have an interest in world peace if they're biting the kids," Cotton said.

"Bertie said they were here first and that the kids needed to learn to coexist with the ants, who have as much right to be here as they do," Gail said glumly.

"Hmm," Cotton said. "We've already crossed the line on that one by not just sitting in the dirt and the rain to have our services. That ship has sailed." He paused for a moment, thinking. "Who did you say the neighbor was now, Shameeka?"

She didn't know the name, but she would go with him to visit if he wanted to go.

"Maybe the neighbors have an interest in treating their fence line for ants!" Gail chimed in, getting the gist quickly.

The next morning Cotton, Gail, and Shameeka climbed the stairs of the neighbors' wooden porch carrying a pink and yellow bag of ant poison. As it turned out, the new neighbor was more than willing for them to pick their way through the brush in the back of his property and scatter the ant poison on his side of the fence where the kids wouldn't be near it, but the ants would have ready access. He was Baptist himself and politely declined an invitation to attend a Sunday service with them. What he said was, "That sounds nice, I'll try to get over there sometime," but everyone knew that in the country around Honey Springs, "I'll try" usually means "no," so they all left knowing what would happen with that.

Gail and Cotton went picking through the brush in the neighbor's yard to spread the bait. Shameeka said yes to a glass of iced tea and kept the neighbor company talking about grandkids while the operation was in progress. They could see Gail and Cotton out the window. It looked as though they were dancing, in a way, stamping their feet and hitting themselves. It was probably good that they couldn't hear them. Craig chose that moment to show up to water the impatiens beds. He nodded to Cotton and Gail across the fence, kept the hose moving, and pretended he didn't know what they were doing. The silence of cumulus clouds filled his head, and he was at peace.

HONEY SPRINGS PLANS A REVIVAL

Rain thudded on the roof and wind tossed the bare branches of the trees outside the windows as the Honey Springs Unitarian Universalist Congregation's Worship Committee sat around the wooden table in Classroom #12. The chalice was lit, and check-in had been accomplished. When it came time to talk about new business, the Rev. Cotton Lovingood, the new minister at the mythical UU congregation where we are all the way we are, only more so, said, "We've been asked to talk about hosting a revival here. Two other congregations want to work on it with us."

"Two other—what kind of congregations?" Jill asked. She was a tall woman, dressed tonight in blue layers with a pattern stamped on the blue with black ink.

"UU congregations," Cotton said. "It's supposed to be a UU revival."

"Revival?" asked Al, a rangy man with bright blue eyes and a full head of white hair. "Isn't that a bit evangelical for us? What are we supposed to do, recite our Principles and shout Hallelujah?"

"Evangelical is something UUs can be about this faith," Cotton said. "We certainly have good news to share, and that's what the word evangelical means."

"Yes," Jill said. "I think we have a lot of good things going on here, and I think we should talk them up a little bit! I mean, just saying 'There is no hell' would be telling the good news, don't you think?"

"I think a revival is an exciting idea," Jim said. Jim pushed his glasses back up onto his nose and smiled at Cotton. "We could have gospel choirs from the church down the street. They would raise the roof on this place! We could get some fired-up preaching and really start appealing to more folks around here."

"Who would that appeal to, though?" Al asked, leaning back in his chair, spreading his hands. "Would we want a bunch of people in here that wanted to whoop and holler and jump around?"

"Al, nobody's talking about jumping around," Cotton said, "although I think you may have pointed up a class issue in this whole concept. The emotional tone of a revival may be uncomfortable to people whose idea of reverence is sitting quietly with hands folded in their laps."

Al looked stung. Cotton had the sneaking suspicion that he should have shut up about the class issue.

"I just think people are tired of our congregations pussyfooting around the word 'God' and feeling afraid to use it for fear of being mocked," Jim said.

"I have to say I'm very uncomfortable with this," Jill said. "It sounds like when we use the word "revival" it makes people think about doing a pale imitation of Christianity here, mining it for its emotional energy or luring people into our congregation with a promise we can't keep. I mean, we're not a Christian church, and if people want Christianity there are 11 million places they can go."

"The imitator dooms himself to hopeless mediocrity," Al said. "Emerson said that in his Divinity School Address. The cure for deformed religion is soul, soul, and again soul. Something like that."

"We do have Christian roots," Jim said, "and I think it would be good to celebrate those."

"We also have Transcendentalist roots," Jill said, her face turning pink, "and the pagan group here celebrates that nature mysticism of our forebears. Maybe we could have a kind of pagan revival."

"I have a question," Phoebe, the retired anthropologist, said, looking up from her laptop. Four expectant faces turned toward her. One never knew what was going to come out of Phoebe's mouth in that crisp British accent. "What is it we would be attempting to revive if we had this revival?"

"Good question," nodded Cotton. The five of them sat contemplating for ten seconds or so.

"We would revive our sense of awe as we stand in this miraculous world," Al said. "That's a religion that's never hurt anyone, never caused a war . . ."

"You can't blame the religion for the things people do in its name," Jim said. "It's human nature to fight and control and conquer. All those new atheist books about how bad God is are only about how bad Christians have been."

"Buddhism is non-harming," Jill spoke up. "It's a very peaceful . . ."

Phoebe leaned toward her and muttered, "Vietnam. Sri Lanka." Jill closed her mouth and sat back in her chair.

"So what would we be reviving?" Cotton said, attempting to bring back the focus of the conversation.

"Our sense of connection to everyone."

"Our sense of responsibility to making the world a better place."

"Oh, I think we are already flagellated with that enough in this church—it's our own UU version of hellfire and brimstone! We need fuel to run on, a way to keep going when what we are doing seems like not enough, when we get weary and guilty."

"I think we also need to revive hope in the capacity of humans for love, for finding the Divine within ourselves, for walking into wholeness."

"Isn't any of this about a sense of God? I want to revive some talk about God."

"I don't think revivals are about talk. Not talk about anything. I think they are for reviving a direct sense of the sacred, of being filled with light and love, about singing openheartedly and including the body in worship—if we are connected with all beings, we can feel that in our bodies as well as our minds and spirits."

"A revival is about feeling the Holy."

"I don't want a lot of God talk. I think that word holds too much pain and baggage for people. Maybe we used to be a Christian denomination, but we're not anymore."

"I think you can talk about God without having to swallow Christianity," Cotton said. "After all, God is not a Christian."

"God is not a Christian!"

"But there are UU Christians."

"And UU Pagans."

"And UU Humanists."

"At the risk of sounding like a broken record, my friends," Cotton said, "I am asking us here at Honey Springs not to think of ourselves as anything hyphenated. Not UU Christians, or UU Pagans, or UU Buddhists. We are UUs. There is room for all of us in this faith. If you love the Christian story, you can be a straight-down-the-line, middle-of-the-road UU. If you love the Goddess and the drum, you can be a middle-of-the-road UU. If you love science or stand in awe of nature or delight in the capacities of the human spirit, you can be a straight-..."

"Watch who you're calling 'straight!'" Phoebe's finger was pointed at him, in good humor.

". . . down-the-middle Unitarian Universalist, okay?" Cotton finished, shooting Phoebe a smile.

That stopped the brainstorming session. Again, Cotton wondered whether he should have spoken. He took comfort in the thought that if he were the pompous bag-of-wind minister he feared being, he would never find himself wondering whether it had been a good thing to speak up.

"Thank you all for thinking about this with me," he said. "To be continued."

"I may want to read that Divinity School Address of Emerson's, Al," Jim said.

"Just Google it," Al said, looking pleased that someone remembered what he'd said.

The meeting ended with each person assigned to ask their friends the "What would we revive?" question and to design some elements of an event that would lift up and energize the joys they each found in their faith. Jim offered Jill his umbrella as they made ready to dash to their cars through the rain.

LOVE TRUCK

❖

I used to love yelling at big SUVs on the road. "You big-butt trucks are the reason we're having to accede to the demands of foreign oil and human-rights abusing fundamentalists!" Those were not my exact words. The actual vocabulary might have been a tinch more salty. I would give SUV drivers a scornful glance as I zipped past in my fuel-efficient Honda. Those were the good old days of righteousness. These days I will begin a soul-satisfying rant at the master-of-the universe Suburban in front of me at the stop light, and then I remember: One of those things is parked in my driveway. Yeah, it's mine. Here's how it happened.

My beloved sister in Texas needed a new car. They were doing very well in their business. Great people, they give a lot of money away; they work with their church resettling refugees from Afghanistan, hauling whole families and their belongings from place to place. They need roomy vehicles. My sister always drives a Suburban. They came to visit us in South Carolina, bought a new Suburban here, where the prices were lower than at home, and gave us their old car. I can't re-sell it and I can't trade it in without seeming to curl my lip at a gift of love. It's a love truck, pure and simple, and when someone gives you a love truck you'd best just hush up and drive it around town. Go on and put liberal bumper stickers on the back. Just live with the jangle, with the incongruity. It's good for you. Life is complicated.

I have a sneaking suspicion that the Karma Fairy is laughing her head off. She is the force that helps tickle, nudge, or blast us out of our self-righteousness. If we scorn something thoughtlessly enough, she will make sure we have an opportunity to squirm and learn a little something. She wants us to lose the scorn, open our hearts, understand that there are reasons we may not be thinking of behind the things people do, that if you think you're clean, you're dreaming.

I have a friend who, whenever someone cuts him off in traffic, says, "Bless his/her heart, s/he probably just got out of the hospital." Now I have to look at the SUV drivers and think to myself: "Her sister probably gave her that car, and it's a love car, so she has to drive it."

I have read that Unitarian Universalists don't have a strong sense of sin. I beg to differ. Following is a list of some UU sins. If you admitted these at coffee hour, there would be some throat-clearing, some uncomfortable fidgeting, maybe even a stern talking-to: driving a big old gas-guzzling SUV, tossing glass and plastic bottles in the trash, belonging to the National Rifle Association, having a potluck at church without a vegetarian option, watching reality TV, throwing a book away, using a word incorrectly, and feeding the kids sugary snacks, just to name a few.

I think people should drive fuel-efficient cars, build green sanctuaries, eat organic food, keep their engines tuned, and go to the dentist regularly. Here is the problem: all of those things cost money. We have to be careful not to be classist in our distaste for old gas-guzzlers, people who eat bad food or use incorrect grammar, or folks who don't have all of their teeth. The Karma Fairy will get busy with us, shaking us out of our gleeful middle-class moral uprightness. She just wants us to be better people. So if you see a Suburban with "Uncommon Denomination," "Peace is Patriotic," and "Only one six-billionth of this is about you" bumper stickers on it, it's me or someone in my family. Just wave.

NEW CHAPTER

"Start in the kitchen," my church administrator said. "Leave yourself one pot, one frying pan, three plates and three glasses. Pack everything else."

She is a born organizer, so I contemplated doing what she said. As you know, contemplation, even for several days in a row, does not get the job done. My stacks of plates, bowls, spoons and knives sat sturdily in their places as they had since my children were in elementary school.

The family is beginning a new chapter. Kiya, and I are living hundreds of miles away from the boys, safely occupied with college and med school. We have left the South and moved to Princeton, New Jersey. We have imagined a life where we will live simply, do our work, ride our bikes, swim, and breathe in and out, where friends and family can come visit, but the daily rhythm is the rhythm of two. What do two people living lightly need more than a few plates, six forks, six spoons? How do you go from householder to gypsy? How do you go from frying pan to feather on the breath of God? What will we need to take with us, I wondered. Do I take my blue and white charms my best friend brought from Greece that protect against the evil eye? Do they even have the evil eye in New Jersey? Never mind. Scratch that question. I packed it.

We didn't want any of the old coffee mugs any more, we didn't want the forks and spoons, we wouldn't need power tools or extra bed frames in our new life, so we had a Big Giant Yard Sale. The oldest folks came first, taking a squint at all of our power tools, garden implements, extension cords, bikes and bed frames. They scored most of the good stuff for prices I would not have agreed to if I'd already had my coffee. The crowd got younger and less canny as the morning wore on. Last came the dilettantes, the amateurs who bargained half-heartedly and loaded up their loot in cars that were not quite big enough for what they'd bought. After the Big Giant yard sale you could almost tell the garage was somewhat emptier.

After that we sold things on Craigslist until we couldn't sell any more, we put up ads in the category of "free stuff." I hit the "send" button on the computer to post the ad, which read: "anyone who comes and cleans out absolutely everything from the basement and the garage gets to keep whatever they find," and within four minutes I had ten people wanting to come over with pickup trucks. I called the first guy who emailed. He came and cleaned out the basement. The second person who emailed came with her daughters and her dad and cleaned out the garage. They got good stuff and we got good space. It was a fine trade.

The boys have their own house now. The older one got married this past summer to a gem of a high school biology teacher, and they all three live together. He studies, keeps bees, works on cars, and studies. My younger son writes songs that will break your heart and sings them with his band all over the South. And he studies too. Now my precious grandfather clock is keeping time for them. They are eating off of Grandmother's china. The Shiraz carpet is glowing softly on their floor. Heirlooms have been passed down.

Deep questions swirl around the moving process: What is important to keep? What is trash? What about our attachments to things by reason of family or sweetness of memory? How do you give away the Scrabble game you all had so much fun playing in those nights years past, arguing over whether rumbersnap was a word, even though it was in the scrabble dictionary, because what human ever actually used that word in conversation? How do you give away the Scruples game during which you realized that this girl was going to be the one your older son would marry? How do you throw away the small sock you found under your younger son's bed, when he now six foot five inches tall and never will be small again? How do you let go of those times, how do you let the mighty oak you were as a daily parent be uprooted by the slow tornado of time? How do you acknowledge that this pain is what happens to those who are luckiest, and that if it did not happen you would have a larger set of sorrows?

What is most difficult for me is not being any more the kind of mother who is needed immediately and daily.   I have left behind the crammed house of responsibility. I see the warm light from its windows as I look back over my shoulder. Laughter rings out from the porch. Someone is catching lightning bugs in the front yard.

My love and I are walking down the road. That house is not for us right now. We carry what we can lift and no more. It's time for a new perspective. Out of my back pocket peeks a small white sock.

ABOUT THE AUTHOR

Meg Barnhouse grew up in North Carolina and Philadelphia. After graduating from Duke University and Princeton Theological Seminary she spent the next chapter of her life in Spartanburg, SC, working first as a college chaplain teaching Public Speaking, Human Sexuality, and World Religions, trying not to get them mixed up. Earning her credentials as a Pastoral Counselor, she ran her own counseling practice while raising her two sons who are now in their twenties. She was active in the community, preaching and teaching in many churches, recording commentaries for NC Public Radio and "Weekend All Things Considered," serving as Interim Minister in several congregations and helping to found the SAFE Homes Network for battered women. Along the way she earned a second-degree black belt in American Karate. She finished up that southern chapter with seven years as the minister of the Unitarian Universalist Church of Spartanburg. After two years as Interim at the Unitarian Universalist Congregation of Princeton, NJ, she now serves as the minister of the First Unitarian Universalist Church of Austin, Texas.

Meg travels nationwide as a speaker, singer/songwriter and humorist. Often her partner, award-winning singer/songwriter and composer Kiya Heartwood accompanies her.

Her books, *Rock of Ages at the Taj Mahal*, *The Best of Radio Free Bubba*, *Waking Up the Karma Fairy*, *Return of Radio Free Bubba*, *Did I Say That Out Loud*? and this one are compilations of stories from the radio and from the *UU World* magazine.

Meg's CD, *July Blue,* is a mix of 12 original songs and 3 stories. The CD, *Mango Thoughts in a Meatloaf Town*, contains more original songs, including *All Will Be Well*. Her newest CD, *Heart of Compassion*, is a collection of Meg reading her favorite stories from her first several books.

www.megbarnhouse.com

Made in the USA
Charleston, SC
12 June 2011